A Gift From --

Building and Preserving Your Wealth

Building and Preserving Your Wealth

A Practical Guide to Financial Planning for Affluent Investors

STEVEN PODNOS, MD, MBA, CFP®

Oakhill Press
Winchester, VA

10 9 8 7 6 5 4 3 2 1

Library of Congress Cataloging-in-Publication Data

Podnos, Steven, 1956-
    Building and preserving your wealth : a practical guide to financial planning for affluent investors / Steven Podnos.
        p. cm.
    ISBN 1-886939-67-5 (alk. paper)
        1. Portfolio management. 2. Investment analysis. 3. Finance, Personal. I. Title.

HG4529.5.P63 2004
332.024--dc22

                                                                    2004056092

Oakhill Press
1647 Cedar Grove Road
Winchester, VA 22603
800-32-books
Printed in the United States of America

ACKNOWLEDGMENTS

Most thanks go to my wife, Mary, who supported me vigorously in my career change, and who gave me the protected time to write this book. Ellen Reid, book shepherd extraordinaire, was invaluable as well in steering me through the various rocks and shoals of having a book published. Also much thanks to Janet Sonder, Lew and Julie Garrish, Khalid and Debbie Sheikh, and Tim and Annabelle Lang—all who were big supporters early on when it counted the most.

TABLE OF CONTENTS

PREFACE

When it comes to making money, America is by far the greatest country in the world. It is the ultimate land of opportunity. Even if you are born into poverty, brains, ambition, and hard work can lead to success and wealth. A large percentage of the "millionaires next door" come from humble beginnings and are truly self-made. They've worked hard to get where they are today, and most have achieved a level of financial security that enables them to have a desirable lifestyle. I consider myself living proof of this bountiful scenario, being a hard-working, self-made, wealthy professional. My grandparents came to this country penniless, and all their children and grandchildren became wealthy and successful.

Working and making money is an enormously gratifying accomplishment. However, holding onto it—and learning all that you need to know to make your money work for you—is an even more complicated and daunting process. Ironically the very thing that makes this country "great"—freedom—is also often what may contribute to one's financial downfall. We are free to make decisions and choose our actions, but we are also faced with many complicated investment options and financial considerations. Sadly, most wealthy individuals are so busy earning their money that they don't have the time or the interest to become investment or financial experts. Lacking the necessary expertise to properly manage their wealth, they often end up making poor choices. Growing and preserving wealth requires time and attention, which for the average person can often seem overwhelming. It was to me.

Once I had finally become successful enough to begin making some important financial decisions, I sought "expert" advice. There was no shortage of investment specialists knocking at my door. They all offered a broad array of products and services designed to help me manage my money and protect my assets. I quickly learned that though some were ethical and helpful, others were self-serving or even dishonest. Unfortunately, distinguishing the good from the bad was often difficult. Most financial advisors that I encountered earned their money by selling me something. They were paid a commission on what they sold, which in my mind created a conflict of interest. How could I trust that they had my best outcome at heart when they were looking out for their own financial interests? I had worked hard to earn my money, and I was determined to hold onto it. I came to the realization that finding someone who was going to care about my money as much as I did would be difficult, and that some education was necessary.

The educational process involved a twenty-year odyssey into the world of investments and financial planning. Somewhat to my surprise, I discovered that I loved it! The world of finance and investing slowly became more enjoyable to me than the practice of medicine. After many years of intensive effort, I received my master's degree in business administration and completed a course of study to become a Certified Financial Planner®. An awareness of the fee-only financial planning profession led to a mid-life career change. Fee-only planners are paid like physicians and dentists—for time and expertise and not for selling anything. I looked forward to being able to help others by offering the kind of impartial advice and guidance that had eluded me. At our firm, Wealth Care LLC, our clients are confident that our only interest is their financial well-being. Our goal is simple: to grow money safely and to protect assets.

As an expert, I'm often asked to recommend a simple, easy-to-read book that provides the successful individual with a comprehensive overview of the important financial considerations they are facing. No such book was available, which led to the product in your hands. As you read this book, notice that I have a strong bias toward simplicity, low-cost methods, and fee-only professional advice.

This book covers all the important basics of sound financial planning and answers the questions that I'm most often asked:

1. Can I beat the market by picking good stocks?

2. What are the best stocks to buy?

3. Should I buy bonds and real estate?

4. How do I protect myself from inflation?

5. How much and what kind of insurance do I need?

6. How much money do I need to retire?

7. How can I protect myself from lawsuits?

8. Who can I trust for advice?

. . . and much more!

Should you want to delve more deeply into any particular subject, a list of suggested readings and Internet sites appears at the end of each chapter. In addition, our firm's Web site, *www.WealthCareLLC.com*, has links to additional information. You may also contact me personally, at *Steve@WealthCareLLC.com*, to discuss your individual financial concerns.

1

What Are Your Goals?

Mary Hill turned to her husband, "Scott, how badly were we hurt by all that tech stock trouble a couple of years ago?" He replied, "pretty bad, but some of the stocks seem to be coming back finally. But, I've had some sleepless nights wondering if we are on track with our savings, and I'm thinking about getting some help."

Y ou have achieved a good income and/or have accumulated wealth. Rather than providing security, this fact may lead to the anxiety of "keeping safe." How do you manage your income and your savings to ensure the good life in the future?

Does this sound like you? You may be a businessperson or professional with years of hard work behind you. Over the years you probably found yourself distracted by the myriad demands of running a business. Employment law, staff relations, worker's compensation issues, payroll taxes, accounting, liability issues, office space, publicity, marketing, and choosing and paying vendors were among the many new facets of life for which you were unprepared. Probably, at the same time, you were also in the early stages of building a family life in a new community.

You sought out help from advisors, peers, partners, and family, and you muddled through. You are probably experienced at what you do at this point, but you still do not know enough about being successful financially. Do you wonder how to invest your money after the debacle of the late 1990s? How do you protect your family and business life from the apparently increasing threat of liability? How do you sort out all of the various competing claims from advisors urging action on a variety of estate and retirement planning issues? How much money do you need to send your children to college, and what is the best way to save this money?

Because you had the advantage of earning a high income or saving enough to have substantial assets, you are an attractive target for all types of "investments" that are mostly beneficial to salespeople. Rest assured, with the right advice, you can achieve financial security by carefully choosing how you spend and save your income. Prudent, disciplined efforts can ensure financial security, and you can avoid unnecessary risks or speculation in the journey to reach your goals.

If you are not already close to retirement, you need to start investing as early as possible to gain the advantages of compounding. This effect is most important in funding your retirement plans because the growth of your investments is untaxed until distribution. Therefore, you make money on all your earnings, not just the after-tax portion.

We review a practical approach to reaching the desired goal of financial security. Each chapter gives you the basic information you need to understand the issues, and to help you deal with your advisors. Each discussion closes with suggestions for more in-depth reading. These chapters can be read independently, or you may want to read the book as a whole.

2

Investing

Mitch B. stopped me on rounds one day several years ago. "Two more years like this, and I'll be able to retire," he beamed. "Like what?" I asked. He went on to relate his very impressive high double-digit gains in the hot tech stocks of the day. He wouldn't hear any negative comments about market history and typical stock valuations. Currently, Mitch is still working with no early retirement plans, and he is no longer talking about his investments.

As you accumulate assets, you face the complex tasks of both protecting them and making them grow. The process of putting your money to work, with the intention of having both your original stake (your principal) and a "reasonable" return on your investment, is what the investing process is about.

For most of us, the options for our investments are in the equity market (stocks) and fixed-income investment market (bonds and CDs). Outside of some real estate you might own, the bulk of your wealth and retirement savings is typically divided in various asset classes in these two categories.

Stocks represent a piece of direct ownership in a company. Bonds represent a debt instrument (a loan) that pays a fixed income (hopefully), but may also appreciate as well if interest rates drop. When investing in stocks, you may derive gain from dividends paid and/or a potential for capital gains through appreciation in the price of the stock. The universe of equity and debt is vast and includes the following investment groups:

U.S. DOMESTIC EQUITIES

Large-Cap Value
Large-Cap Growth
Small-Cap Value
Small-Cap Growth

INTERNATIONAL (DEVELOPED) EQUITIES

EMERGING MARKETS

FIXED-INCOME INVESTMENTS

Government
Corporate
High-Yield
International
Emerging-Market

BASICS OF EQUITY INVESTMENT

Choices in Ownership

The investor or portfolio manager has several ways to invest in the stock market. Buying individual stocks has the advantage of total control as to which companies are owned, when they are bought, and how long they are owned. The investment expense of owning individual stocks is the transaction costs when they are bought and sold (escaping the yearly overhead of a mutual fund). The manager may also time the harvesting of gains and losses to maximize return. A downside to owning individual stocks is the requirement of having the knowledge of which stocks to buy, and knowing when to sell and what to buy to rebalance the portfolio. Selecting individual equities is the most time- and knowledge-intensive style of investing. The risk of individual company financial distress can be partially mitigated by owning several dozen stocks in diverse industries.

To escape some of the problems inherent in investing in individual stocks, the concept of mutual funds was introduced early in the twentieth century. Mutual funds come in two types. *Closed-end funds* represent a group of stocks that can change, but you purchase a percentage of the entire group. Shares of closed-end funds are bought and sold on an exchange much like an individual equity. These proportional investments can actually trade above or below the true "worth" of the underlying stocks owned by the fund, allowing for some potential gain or loss in a separate fashion. A more popular type of mutual fund is the *open-end fund*. In this case, the fund company issues and redeems shares on a daily basis. When more money is added to the fund, more stocks are bought, and vice versa. The value of the fund is adjusted daily based on the worth of all the underlying stocks owned, divided by the number of fund shares. Most closed-end and open-end funds are actively managed, but almost all index (passive) funds are open-end only.

Mutual funds have the advantage of passive participation on the part of the investor. The only decision is when to sell or buy the fund. Passive index funds have a low cost (see below for no-load funds), but actively managed funds have a significant expense "drag" on a yearly basis. Mutual funds also offer the strong advantage of diversification across the asset class picked.

Growth versus Value Equities

A perennial debate exists among investors and academics about whether to invest in growth or value stocks. Growth stocks are equities of companies that are thought to have the potential to sustain a rapid growth in future earnings. These stocks typically pay little to no dividend income and have a high "valuation" when factors such as stock price to book value, or price to earnings, are considered. Value stocks are the ugly ducklings, thought to be stodgy and dull. They pay a higher dividend and tend to be less volatile. In most studies, value wins out over the long term, although certainly in some periods of years one style of investing predominates (growth trounced value from 1997 to 2000, and now [in 2004] value is winning). This fact argues again for diversification into both growth and value sectors rather than trying to catch the trend just right.

International Investing

When our financial news is focused on domestic markets, forgetting the rest of the world is easy. However, more than half of the world's stock market capitalization exists outside our borders. Most of this wealth is concentrated in the well-developed countries of Europe and in Japan, with a lesser amount scattered among the emerging markets of less-well-developed areas. Two emerging markets are actually the two most populous countries in the world, India and China.

International investments do not necessarily perform better than domestic stocks in the long term. However, they offer the advantage (discussed in more detail later) of some differences in correlation. Even though some large-capitalization European stocks are beginning to act much like our own large domestic stocks, in general, having some international stocks (especially from emerging markets) seems like a prudent part of diversification in an asset allocation program.

An additional factor to consider in international investing is that of currency risk. In addition to the relative performance of a foreign stock, the investor must monitor the relative value of that country's currency to the U.S. dollar. Ultimately we want our money back in dollars, and some mutual funds therefore hedge the currency risk using specialized financial devices known as derivatives.

Foreign markets are not as efficient as our own. They have different accounting standards and different levels of press scrutiny. Some emerging markets have a long history of frequent insider trading, and others restrict the amount of stock that foreigners can own. These latter facts have led some advisors to suggest that active managers may have an edge over passive investors in these less efficient markets.

Exchange-Traded Funds

Exchange-traded funds (ETFs) are very much like index mutual funds in that both attempt to passively own all the stocks in a particular group or index. You may have heard of the "QQQ," representing the NASDAQ's one hundred largest stocks, or "Spyders," representing the S&P 500. ETFs differ from index mutual funds in that they are bought and sold on an exchange with a commission for each transaction. They generally offer very low yearly expenses as compensation for their transaction costs. They allow moving into and out of indexes with ease, whereas some index mutual funds make this flexibility difficult. No-load index funds might be a better vehicle for frequent or small investments, to avoid the brokerage commissions associated with ETFs. This method of investing in equities and bonds is a useful option for the portfolio manager, and the popularity of ETFs is growing rapidly.

INVESTING STYLE

Can You Invest by Yourself?

You can certainly invest your own funds and follow them with a relatively small time commitment each month. However, the process of investing requires a disciplined, steady approach year after year, which is much harder than it sounds. In addition, as discussed below, another important feature of disciplined investing involves moving funds from asset classes that are doing well into those asset classes that are lagging behind. The average do-it-yourself investor finds this process exceedingly difficult. Letting the winners run is much easier, only to hold them too long. This section offers some guidelines on either investing by yourself or helping you to understand what your advisor is thinking about as he or she invests your funds.

Active versus Passive Investing

The financial literature relates several decades of debate on whether or not "active" management is superior to "passive" management. Active management implies that a fund, hedge, or separate-account manager actively picks among stocks (or bonds) in a particular area (or "sector"), trying to beat the return of owning all the choices in that sector. For example, an active large-cap fund manager picks from the universe of large-capitalization (multibillion-dollar company) stocks in an attempt to beat the return of a large-cap index. This index is a calculated measure of price movement of all of the stocks in that sector. For example, a reasonably well-known index for large-cap stocks is the S&P 500. This particular index is a slowly changing compilation of five hundred large-company stocks picked by a private financial services firm, Standard and Poor's.

The debate over active vs. passive investing centers on whether the active manager is smart enough to use generally available information in an attempt to consistently outperform the index in which he or she invests. The evidence is convincing that in highly traded markets, it is extremely difficult to beat the market over time by picking individual securities. The active manager must not only pick well, but must also overcome the significantly higher costs of the fund (salaries, commissions, marketing, profits, etc.) year after year. Finally, even if you believe that some rare managers can beat the market over long periods of time, do you think that you can pick out those managers in advance?

Why, then, are most individuals invested in active funds?

First, investments are sold more than they are bought. There is a much lower potential profit available for managing or for selling a commodity-like index fund, as these funds compete only on cost. Active management carries the cachet and hope of outperforming the index.

Also, we are optimistic. Aren't all our children above average? Aren't we all better-than-average drivers? Well, aren't we also better "pickers" of funds than the poor average guy?

Finally, the financial press drives our decision-making process. If there were only index funds, the business pages would consist of a few lines in the back of the newspaper reporting the indexes' performances. The financial press lives off touting "The Ten Best Stocks" or "The Best Managers of the Year," despite the repeated evidence that this information harms the investors. The sizzle and appeal of "beating the market" sells well.

Now, having said that it does not work, we should note that active management might be preferable in certain circumstances. Remember that active management does not work in highly *efficient*, well-analyzed markets like the S&P 500. By definition, an *inefficient* market does not have widespread dissemination of information, so that a person willing to do some detective and analytical work might pick a jewel from the rocks. Inefficient markets that might allow an advantage to active managers include emerging markets and small-capitalization domestic stocks, as well as high-yield corporate bonds. In these areas a good active manager might be able to gain some advantage through diligent work. Still, the active managers in question must overcome the "drag" of the higher expenses year after year, and the evidence that they can do so is sparse.

Another time to consider active management is when there are recognized occasional gross market inefficiencies in both broad markets and in specific sector stocks. These aberrations should be noticed and acted on in the investment process. For example, by early 2000, a student of the market would have noted a historically unsustainable rise in the price of most stocks, especially in the tech sector. Similarly, in 2003–4, the historic twenty-year bull market in bonds appears ready to end, as interest rates are seemingly too low in a monetary system that ultimately favors inflation. Owning a passive index of overpriced stocks is not a winning method of investing.

For a few asset classes, index funds are not yet easily available. In these classes, such as commodities and some natural resources, active management might be your best or only choice.

At times, there may be some confusion as to how much real correlation exists between an actively managed fund and its comparative index. Perhaps the fund manager is not really investing in the exact type of stocks represented by the index he is compared to (more and more likely, depending on how esoteric the index is). When evaluating an active manager, research the investment style of the fund before drawing conclusions about its performance compared to a particular index.

The Importance of Diversification

The process of investment management actually always has an active component, in deciding which asset classes to invest in as well as how much of one's portfolio goes into each asset class. This decision-making process is usually guided by an economic science known as Modern Portfolio Theory (MPT). MPT teaches that holding a group of assets that do not strongly correlate with each other's performance leads to less volatility and better portfolio returns. Therefore, the process of building a portfolio involves determining which of the many possible asset classes should be present and in what percentage. Although some controversy over this theory remains, asset allocation is still felt to be the major determinant of portfolio returns (when compared with market timing and individual security selection). The knowledge needed to determine which asset classes are necessary for proper diversification is one of the value-added attributes of the professional investment manager. Too often, well-known mutual funds all invest heavily in the same popular stocks, leading to portfolio concentration. This condition was clearly present in the great bear market of 2000–2002 when most investors found out that their mutual funds were all heavily concentrated in the same high-technology stocks, regardless of the funds' description.

Investors need to remember that over long periods of time equities provide a higher but more volatile return than do interest-bearing investments over long periods of time. Therefore, a long time horizon is necessary to smooth out this volatility and capture the long-term "risk premium" of equities.

SPECIFIC RECOMMENDATION FOR EQUITY INVESTMENTS

The investor should first make a *strategic* asset allocation—the process of choosing which asset classes should make up parts of the portfolio. At the same time, the approximate percentage of the total portfolio that each asset class contributes is determined.

In most cases, passive low-cost vehicles such as index funds and exchange-traded funds should be used to own these asset classes. Some advisors modify this approach and add an active manager(s) who excels in an inefficient market sector. This process should also recognize when certain market segments are abnormally expensive or cheap based on historical returns and valuation. Within these strategic allocations are *tactical* "limits" to the percentage of investments in each sector that would trigger rebalancing transactions. The rebalancing process ensures that your portfolio won't become too concentrated in the hot sectors, and simultaneously has a reasonable allocation in the unloved sectors (expected to do well in the future).

The portfolio requires regular but not daily or even weekly review.

A reasonable portfolio should include a majority tilt toward equities unless your time horizon is ten years or less. The longer your time horizon, the more stocks you should have in the portfolio.

When interest rates are historically low (as in late 2003), your fixed-income investments should be in short-term or in high-yield bonds. High-yield bonds ("junk bonds") are corporate securities issued by companies who either do not pay to have their debt reviewed or have some financial difficulties. Their higher rate of default compared to rated bonds is usually exceeded by their higher overall return and interest yield. They also are less responsive in a downward sense to rising interest rates. Short-term bonds are also less volatile in reaction to interest-rate hikes, as you receive your principal back before the effect of the higher rates does much damage. With a background of higher interest rates, the length (or term to maturity) of your fixed-income investments can increase to capture a higher interest rate return. In most cases, unless you are certain that interest rates will be falling, it is prudent to avoid bonds with the longest maturities.

Four very important concepts of investing are those of *risk, diversification, time horizon,* and *cost.* Risk is not a pejorative term, but merely a reflection that stock values and returns are volatile. Volatility is a pleasure in an up market, but painful in reverse. However, this variability of return is a stronger presence in certain equities than in others. For example, small companies (small-cap stocks) are more volatile in price and performance than are large companies. Also, stocks that pay small or no dividends are almost always more volatile than stocks that pay large dividends. Accordingly, the price of large groups of small-cap stocks and of stocks that pay no dividends (growth companies) is more volatile than the price of large groups of large companies. The important thing to know is that *in general, a higher risk or volatility leads to a higher long-term return.* The patient investor is paid to take on the additional risk, which makes sense. Who would buy the riskier stock of a small company instead of the alternative of a large "safe" company, unless there was the expectation of a higher return over time?

The prudent investor capitalizes on this risk-and-return relationship by favoring equities in an investment portfolio. The more risk an investor is willing to assume, the more tilted the portfolio is toward equities in general. Even more short-term risk can be assumed by investing in more volatile sectors of equities (emerging markets, small-cap stocks).

Closely tied to the concept of risk/volatility is the time horizon an investor is able to use. The very nature of volatility means that the price of an investment can swing higher and lower through periods of time. The prudent investor realizes this and allocates only those funds that can wait out the downswings in volatile investments in order to reap the higher gains. Practically speaking, you should have a time horizon for equity investing that is measured in decades and not in single years. Money that you need liquid for any purpose in fewer than 10 years should probably not be in equities. If you can commit the funds for longer periods of time, you should capitalize on this fact by allocating a large proportion of your investments to equities.

Diversification of your investments is a way to increase return and decrease risk simultaneously. We reviewed that risk and volatility (often the same thing) are proportional to return over long periods. Interestingly, different asset classes have their own volatilities over time, and many of these moves don't occur at the same points in time (that is, they are not well correlated).

The amount of correlation between asset classes helps the portfolio manager smooth out the overall return. For example, real estate investments do not tend to move up and down in any real relation to what the stock market is doing. A portfolio that contains both real estate and stock would be considered to have poorly correlated asset classes (a good thing, even though it sounds bad). When the stock market is rising, the real estate portion might be rising, stay flat, or actually fall, and vice versa. A balanced collection of assets (well diversified in terms of correlations) usually has some asset classes rising and some falling in price (not the same as value in all instances). This diversification leads to a higher rate of return and investment success with a long-time horizon.

One caution on diversification is necessary. The investor or portfolio manager must see the entire spectrum of a portfolio's investments to avoid false diversification. You might own several mutual funds that actually include mostly the same stocks. You might own similar investments allocated in different accounts (IRA, pension plan, personal assets) and not realize that you have too much money concentrated in the same asset class.

The final, but no less important, concept to understand is the effect of investment expenses. Every penny spent in the process of investing comes out of your pocket and directly diminishes your portfolio's return. Make sure you are getting your money's worth. A good financial planner is worth the expense by helping you stay invested in a diversified and disciplined manner. In addition, the advisor should be helping with financial issues not directly related to investing. Until the evidence proves otherwise, you should not pay for any active management of investments in fixed-income or large, efficient stock markets. In these asset classes use low-cost no-load index funds or ETFs. Some allocation to active managers may be worthwhile in inefficient markets (emerging markets, small-cap stocks), but a good argument can be made to index these as well. In most cases, yearly expenses for these choices are less than 0.5 percent of assets.

The issue of cost is vital for your financial outcome. Even index funds sold by stockbrokers have much higher costs and/or loads. One common arrangement at brokerage firms is to offer a wrap account. With these accounts you are told you can buy stocks and funds at no commission for "only" a yearly fee averaging over 2 percent. If long-term returns from the stock market are in single digits, these expenses are catastrophic. Find a fee-only advisor with reasonable expenses to help you invest in low-cost funds.

We have learned that a portfolio invested long-term—tilted toward equities and having some poorly correlated asset classes—is likely to provide financial success. We also learned that volatility works both ways, and this knowledge might influence asset choices in a diversified portfolio. A manager looking to rebalance a portfolio or to add new money should consider investing in those asset classes that are not performing well, with the anticipation that they will cycle back up in time.

ODDS AND ENDS IN EQUITY INVESTING

Separate Accounts

Think of separate accounts as small mutual funds. For these investments, a fund manager agrees to manage a group of stocks for you, theoretically paying attention to your tax situation and investing style. Once the arena of the extremely wealthy, they are now offered in beginning investment amounts as small as $25,000.

These investments should be approached with caution. They are being marketed as the "next great new thing." They do not have much of a track record and are just another layer of expense (much like an actively managed mutual fund). If you feel the need to have some actively managed equity investments in your portfolio, you would be better off with a mutual fund manager with a long-term track record.

Hedge Funds

Most investors should resist the glamour of hedge funds. These funds are run by active managers who believe they can beat the market returns by using a combination of strategies including selling stocks short (selling unowned stock with the intention of buying it back when it drops lower). They have high expenses and are difficult to monitor in terms of long-term performance. Leave hedge funds to highly sophisticated investors. You don't need the additional risk they entail to have financial success.

FIXED-INCOME INVESTMENTS

Remember that a fixed-income investment is the act of lending another entity (usually a company or the government) your money. In exchange, you expect and hope for a return of your investment later with some interest proportional to the risk and time involved. You do not participate in the upside of a company, but may suffer from the downside. You might ask, therefore, why own bonds (the most common fixed-income choice)? One reason is to capture a steady return on your investment without the volatility of the equity markets, which is especially important if you have a short or intermediate need to have your principal back intact. A second reason to own debt instruments is to provide diversification in the event of an equity market catastrophe.

Remember two important concepts when investing in bonds. First, think about the length of time that you are agreeing to loan out your funds. The length of time you give someone else your money exposes you to the risk of interest rate and inflation changes. The second concept to review carefully is how likely you are to get your money back (the credit risk).

In general, short-term investments are safer. Logically, with all other things being equal, over short periods of time there is less chance of an event leading to an inability to pay you back your investment. There is also less interest rate risk (rising rates), as you are getting back your money quickly and can reinvest it for a higher yield. In an environment of falling interest rates you would be better off in a longer-term investment. Usually, but not all the time, short-term investments pay a lower rate of return, which is reflective of their lower risk.

As the length of time (maturity) of your loan increases, you take on more risk that things may change in the borrower's status and subsequent ability to pay. In addition, you increase the risk that interest rate changes may affect both the worth of your underlying principal and the value of your interest income stream. For example, inflation that is higher than predicted can both erode the value of your principal when you get it back and reduce the value of the interest stream you receive.

To illustrate, before you buy a 30-year bond yielding 5 percent annually from a large corporation, you must consider several factors. First, you must decide whether the company is likely to survive and pay not only your interest income, but return your principal in 30 years. Next, you must decide whether current interest rates are likely to go up or down (or both) over 30 years. If interest rates rise, two unfortunate things happen to your investment. First, the value of the bond drops (if you need to sell it), as a buyer expects a higher rate of return from the fixed interest payments. If interest rates rise to 10 percent, the buyer would want to pay only a little more than half of what you paid in order to get a 10 percent return ($50 a year on a $1,000 bond). Second, you earn relatively less interest on your investment. On your old bond, you would be making 5 percent a year for many more years, when new money is making 10 percent. Finally, with a higher-than-expected rate of inflation and a rise in interest rates, your principal will be worth much less in 30 years than it started out to be. Also with inflation, the income stream you are receiving is fixed and worth less every year with inflation.

All of the above is true in reverse if inflation recedes and interest rates drop. This is what has happened over the last two decades, producing one of the great bond bull markets in history. The rate of return on long-term bonds for the last twenty years has roughly equaled the return of equities, a situation that is very unusual. As discussed elsewhere, knowing that this bond bull market has been long and sustained, and that interest rates are unusually low, it would be wise to consider not having long-term bonds in one's portfolio as of this writing (2004). The downside looms much larger than the upside.

The second aspect of bond investing is how credit worthy the investment is. The U.S. government is considered a risk-free borrower, as it is able to print money and raise taxes in order to repay its debts. All other borrowers have some risk of default and offer a higher rate of interest in compensation. While ratings agencies assess a borrower's ability to repay debt, the risk of individual company distress is always something to consider, and not usually obvious. Debt holders of Enron and WorldCom probably slept well until near the end for both companies. Higher-rated bonds carry a lower rate of interest, reflecting their lesser risk of default. Those companies that are most likely to default issue bonds considered "junk" or high-yield, which pay a much higher rate of interest to compensate for the possibility that you might lose your money. When investing outside of U.S. government securities, consider bond funds of varying maturity (rather than individual bonds) in order to spread out the risk of individual company problems.

OTHER INVESTMENT CHOICES

Real Estate

You probably already have a real estate investment in your portfolio in the form of your home. Our residence also provides some asset protection, depending on the state in which we live. Many planners feel that this ownership gives the individual more than enough exposure to this segment of the investing spectrum, and as such avoid any other real estate investments in a portfolio. Other planners feel that some exposure to real estate through real estate investment trusts (REITs) provides exposure to a different segment of the real estate market (usually commercial property and apartment buildings) and is a reasonable investment despite ownership of local real estate. This asset class also usually helps with dividing your portfolio among noncorrelated classes.

Many of you may invest in other real estate in the form of a second home or local commercial property. This investment can be good financially, but is usually time consuming and requires some patience and knowledge. These types of investments can offer a reasonable return on your money, and a section at the back of the book covers some of the issues involved when owning second homes.

Collectibles

Collectibles are almost never a good investment. Treat them as a hobby or avocation. Do not count on them to provide for your old age unless you have some very specialized knowledge in a particular field. Enjoy them, and invest elsewhere.

Speculation

We all have our temptations and experiences relating to speculation. In fact, probably there is nothing terribly wrong with gambling or speculation in moderation. However, the readers of this book are fortunate in that they can achieve financial security without taking on speculative risk. Accordingly, why would you want to risk losing a virtually guaranteed long-term success by speculating? Is the potential additional gain (short or long term) worth the possibility of losing your security?

Do not succumb to the lure of large speculative investments that can result in a significant financial shortfall. Although you may have many years to "make it up," the money you lose could have become a great fortune if invested prudently. Confine your speculation to small, insignificant ventures such as a short stay in Las Vegas or a small investment in a stock that you think looks good. Consider speculation as part of your entertainment budget and not an investment.

Commodities/Natural Resources

Commodities such as iron, copper, aluminum, wheat, and other tangible items offer an interesting source of diversification for your portfolio. However, investing in this asset class comes with problems. Only a few mutual funds offer exposure to natural resources such as gold, oil, natural gas, and silver, and almost no funds offer exposure to the wide spectrum of commodities in general. Additionally, non-energy-related commodities have had a century-long bear market, usually becoming cheaper and more available as technological advances occur. Just the same, many advisors (including myself) believe that this asset class should be part of any diversified portfolio when possible.

SUMMING IT ALL UP

- Invest in a diversified manner with several asset classes always present in your portfolio. Invest in equities primarily if you have at least ten years to ride out the effects of volatility in your accounts.

- Use low-cost index funds and ETFs to invest in each asset class.

- Rebalance your portfolio at least yearly. Take some funds from those asset classes that have done well, and put them into the asset classes that have lagged behind.

- Find a fee-only financial planner, preferably a Certified Financial Planner®. Let the planner do the work, and enjoy the rest of your life!

REFERENCES ON INVESTING

www.EfficientFrontier.com. A quarterly journal written by investment guru/neurologist William Bernstein M.D. His articles are somewhat academic, but very well written.

The Four Pillars of Investing by William Bernstein. McGraw Hill. This book makes the case for modern portfolio theory and for using index-type investments. It is an excellent read as well.

A Random Walk down Wall Street by Burton Malkiel. W. W. Norton & Company. One of the early advocates of low-cost index investing. Updated every few years.

Common Sense on Mutual Funds by John Bogle. Written by the founder of Vanguard Funds, a pithy, nononsense review of the case for no-load index investing.

What Has Worked in Investing. A Tweedy Browne manuscript available at *www.tweedy.com/content .asp?pageref=investment.* An exceptional review of the case for active management using value-type stocks.

www.IShares.com. This site has much in the way of educational material on exchange traded funds.

www.investinginbonds.com. Great site for information on the bond market.

www.thestreet.com. This always entertaining Web site has multiple daily online columns on many aspects of investing and finance.

www.indexfunds.com/home.php. Links to many good articles on the reasons to use index funds.

3

Retirement Planning

Harry B. sat in the physicians' lounge eating lunch. He was telling a couple of colleagues about his upcoming retirement plans: a life of golf, sun, and relaxation. I thought it unlikely that this hard-driving, Type A surgeon would readily adapt to such a schedule, especially since he had never played golf!

*H*ow do you picture your retirement years? Many dream of the day ahead in which they can stay home, or play tennis and golf all day. In his book *The New Retirementality*, author Mitch Anthony aptly pointed out, however, that few of us are going to be happy or satisfied with a life of only leisure. In achieving your success, you became used to a stimulating and challenging existence, and are not likely to be happy filling your hours with simple pursuits. Most of us need a continuing intellectual challenge and a meaningful, productive life well past what is considered the normal retirement age.

There are several possible paths toward a satisfying "retirement." Some of you would enjoy a continuation of your current occupation as long as possible. We all have seen individuals work well into their seventh and eighth decades, maintaining enthusiasm and a quality of life that is to be envied. For others, a modification of work might be the answer. Perhaps you will work fewer hours per week and take more vacations. Perhaps instead you will take on an actual change in work responsibilities. Similar options exist in a move toward continuing a slightly different approach to your career and skills. A physician might work part-time for a cruise ship. A businesswoman might entertain a career as a consultant for start-up companies.

Another path in retirement might involve a major career change. Hearing about medical and dental professionals studying law and/or business is increasingly common. Physicians are finding themselves in demand for administrative positions at pharmaceutical and health care organizations. Scores of ex-corporate and ex-government employees are starting second careers in mid-life. Although many of these second occupations build on the years of experience the individual has, other choices may have nothing to do with the individual's prior responsibilities.

Your actual activity in later years will have a strong influence on the need for asset accumulation in the working years. Considering your day-to-day existence when planning the retirement years is of vital importance. A future occupation that is income producing requires less need for savings. Part of counseling a client for retirement involves the mutual discovery of what retirement actually means, both in psychosocial and financial terms.

HOW LONG WILL MY MONEY LAST?

You continue to be an investor until the very end of your life. With average life expectancies approaching nine decades, retirement at age fifty-five might mean the need for another thirty years of an income stream. A multitude of studies have tried to determine how much of one's assets can be consumed without running out of money. The consensus is that you can likely withdraw 4 percent of your net assets each year without too much concern about running dry. This is a rough guide, and you should reassess your asset base and spending habits periodically.

SOURCES OF INCOME IN RETIREMENT

When you begin a change in your work life, you may have several sources of income. Aside from any income you might still be earning by working, your need for money will be met by consuming your savings and the earnings on them. These savings fall into two categories: pretax and post-tax. Post-tax funds are funds that are not in a pension plan or IRA.

Some assets may have a partial post-tax basis, as is the case in a nondeductible IRA. With such an IRA, withdrawal of the earnings are taxable, but the amount of your contributions that were after-tax money is considered a withdrawal of your principal and is not taxed again. Similarly, a deferred annuity (discussed in a later chapter) pays out a mixture of taxable and non-taxable income. Your office and/or home might also provide a source of significant untaxed principal from which to invest or spend.

Pretax funds are those that you saved in one or more of the various retirement funds discussed below.

SOCIAL SECURITY

Despite the fact that you have paid Social Security taxes for decades, it is unlikely to be a significant source of income in retirement (unless you are at least in your sixth decade or older already). The income from Social Security payments is already highly taxed if you have any other significant income. Many advisors have grave doubts about whether this program will really provide any meaningful support in the future for any but the poor. Assume that you will have access to Social Security disability support (discussed in another chapter), but not a meaningful contribution to your retirement needs.

Qualified Retirement Plans

The term "qualified" refers to the government's approval of the terms and limitations of a retirement plan. In exchange for meeting these rules, you are granted a tax-deferred status on most contributions and all earnings until withdrawal. These government controls seek to ensure that the wealthy don't have too much advantage over lower-income coworkers and employees.

An important point to make is that all retirement plans fall into the category of either a *defined contribution* or a *defined benefit plan*. The vast majority of plans involve a defined contribution. In these programs a contribution is made to the plan (usually yearly), but the benefit derived from the savings is a function of the amount saved and the investment experience. There are no guarantees as to how much money will be available for retirement. In a defined benefit plan the employer assumes the risk of contributing enough to have a guaranteed amount at retirement, regardless of the investment experience. The significant risk associated with this guarantee is behind the shift from defined benefit to defined contribution in most firms. The vast majority of qualified plans in business and the professions use a defined contribution method.

Defined Contribution Plans

IRAs. The basic retirement account available to every worker (and spouse) is the Individual Retirement Account. In 2004 (at the time of this writing), most Americans can contribute $3,000 a year ($3,500 for those over fifty) to their own IRA. These accounts are not technically "qualified" plans, and do not offer strong asset protection in every state. A pretax contribution is always possible if neither you nor your spouse participate in another qualified plan, regardless of your income. If either of you do participate in a qualified plan, then strict income limitations determine whether your IRA contribution is a pretax item or not.

Earnings on your IRA funds are not taxed until you begin to make withdrawals. At that point, the withdrawals are taxed in proportion to how much after-tax money was contributed. For example, if all of your contributions were made pretax, every dollar of your withdrawals is taxed as ordinary income. If some of your contributions were made with after-tax money, a formula determines the percentage of your withdrawals that will be taxed. All tax on IRA withdrawals is in the ordinary income category. You may generally not withdraw IRA funds before age 59½ except for several specific reasons beyond the scope of this chapter (see the references for details). You must begin required distributions at age 70½. The laws determining what happens to the undistributed funds at your death are very complex, and you should review this with your advisors.

A few years ago, the Roth IRA was introduced for those families with less than $150,000 of gross income yearly. In this case, after-tax contributions are made to the IRA, but all earnings and withdrawals come out tax-free. If you are interested, see the references at the end of the chapter.

A final IRA is the Coverdell IRA, formerly known as the Educational IRA. More on this topic is available in the section on educational planning as it is not really a retirement vehicle.

Simplified Employee Pensions (SEPs). In a SEP the employer makes contributions to his or her own individual retirement account (IRA) as well as the IRAs of employees, subject to certain percentages of pay and dollar limits. Contributions can be determined on a year-by-year basis, and the plans are easy and inexpensive to operate. You can put as much as 25 percent of your compensation into a SEP-IRA (capped at $41,000 a year in 2004). These plans are attractive in their simplicity, but are costly because of the need to compensate employees with the same "percentage" of income that you use to maximize your contribution. Some of the other plan choices usually come out less expensive for the employer (although more complicated to initiate and administer). If you have very few employees, consider a SEP, but seek an expert opinion.

Simple IRAs. A bridge between a 401(k) plan *(see below)* and the SEP, this plan uses combined contributions from the employer and employee to fund the employee's IRA. There are more severe limits on total contributions allowed than most of the other plans discussed here. Simple IRAs are designed for small companies.

401(k) Plans. These very popular plans utilize employee salary (pretax) contributions of up to $13,000 yearly (more for people over fifty). Employers may match employee contributions and can also contribute a percentage of income as a profit-sharing addition to these plans. Several permutations allow a maximization of contributions for employers while minimizing the cost of contributions for employees. The 401(k) is a very common model of retirement plans for business and professional corporations.

Profit-Sharing Plans. These once-popular defined contribution plans are being replaced by or combined with 401(k) plans. A profit-sharing plan allows a percentage of the first $200,000 of income to be the pretax contribution. Having the first $13,000 of plan contributions coming from employee salary deferral (in the 401[k]) allows a much smaller percentage of income required to fund the remainder. For this reason, most new plans will probably use the 401(k) model or shared model rather than the profit-sharing plan alone.

Money Purchase Plans. A now-antiquated but also once-popular defined contribution plan, the money purchase plan called for a rigid fixed percentage of compensation to be used for the yearly plan amount. Money purchase plans were used in the past to maximize employer contributions, as profit-sharing contributions were limited. With recent tax law changes, these plans are no longer needed, and the IRS has made it relatively easy to merge them into profit-sharing plans.

Defined Benefit Plans

In a defined benefit plan, you are guaranteeing a certain benefit to your employees in the distant future, regardless of how well you invest and contribute. In addition, these plans are complex and expensive to administer. The yearly contribution is calculated annually by an actuary, and the risk of poor investment performance to the employer (usually you) is high.

Certain circumstances make these plans very interesting. Specifically, an employer in the fifth or sixth decade of life with young employees can make a proportionally huge contribution at levels that far exceed the usual limits of defined contribution plans. Because the defined benefit plan promises a benefit, the actuary can figure out how much needs to be saved in a relatively small number of years to ensure this amount. It is not unusual for an employer in this setting to be able to put away more than $100,000 a year (pretax) during the last decade of work. These plans almost never make sense before this age.

A new twist to defined benefit plans is known as the 412(i). This plan uses life insurance to fund plan benefits, and is therefore understandably being sold aggressively. Suffice it to say that these plans have fallen under recent IRS scrutiny. Caveat emptor.

COMMENT

No two businesses or professional practices are exactly alike. The determinants of what retirement plan would work best for you include income levels, the ratio of owners to staff, and the ages of participants. It would be well worth your time to discuss this very important topic with an expert before making up your mind.

If you have an existing plan, you must keep up with IRS regulations and plan revisions. A prototype plan run by a national brokerage or pension firm will simultaneously make the necessary changes to the plan for all their clients. However, this "one size fits all" prototype plan may not fit your needs. In this case, you will need a custom written plan and a third party administrator and legal firm to keep you up to date. Which one makes sense for you is a decision you need to make after becoming informed.

REFERENCES ON RETIREMENT PLANNING

http://flagship3.vanguard.com/web/planret/Planning AdvicePublicOverview.html. The Vanguard Funds site has several good articles on retirement planning and investing.

The Retirement Savings Time Bomb . . . and How to Defuse It by Ed Slott. A newly published book with much more than you ever wanted to know about IRAs.

J. K. Lasser's Your Winning Retirement Plan by Henry K. Hebeler. A good general review of the types of plans as well as some investing advice.

The New Retirementality by Mitch Anthony. Referenced in the chapter, an eye-opening discussion on what retirement really entails.

4

Educational Planning

Sally G. called her best friend Lauren to give her the good news about her oldest daughter. "Jill was accepted to Duke!" she crowed. "Fantastic," said Lauren, "but how are you going to pay for that on your salary?" Sad, but true, Sally was still not a partner in the dental practice and had been able to save very little toward Jill's education.

O ther than your home, your children's college education will be the most expensive purchase you make. In almost all instances, saving for this goal should begin when the children are small. If you have achieved some financial success, it may prevent your children from receiving any financial aid. However, you might have just enough wealth to disqualify your family from aid, but not enough to pay the expense of several years at a university.

The amount that you need to save is determined by in a multistep approach. First, determine the estimated cost per year of the college or graduate school you expect the child to attend. If your child is small, you must also account for the yearly rise in educational costs that currently exceeds the rate of general inflation. Second, estimate how many years of school you expect to pay for. Finally, consider collateral sources of funding, such as support from grandparents. There are college savings calculators available in the references at the end of the chapter, and your advisor should be able to help you as well.

Several ways are available to save for your children's education. Of note is that the only way to use pretax money for this purpose is to have your child fund a traditional IRA *(see below)*.

INDIVIDUAL SAVINGS

Some couples elect to keep a (mentally or physically) segregated amount of their savings dedicated toward educational costs. This approach has the advantage of the funds remaining under your control. However, discipline is needed to separate the money from other assets so that it will be truly available when needed. Any taxable earnings on these accounts will be taxed in the parents' bracket.

UTMA ACCOUNTS

Gifting money to children and setting up these accounts is a legal transfer to the child. At age eighteen or twenty-one (depending on the age of majority in your state) they are able to take all this money and do with it as they please (hopefully for an education). You are not technically allowed to spend this money on the normal support of the child, but could use it for extras such as automobile and entertainment costs if it became desirable to "spend down" this money before age eighteen. These accounts are considered the child's assets for financial aid matters. A positive aspect of these accounts is that they allow you to benefit from the lower income taxes on the first $1,500 of unearned income that the child derives from investments each year.

529 PLANS

These state-run plans have become a popular and powerful method of educational savings. There are actually two types of 529 plans. The first type of plan is the prepaid tuition plan. An amount is determined (based on your child's current age) that will guarantee a credit for tuition for up to four years. A separate contract can be used to purchase dormitory costs in some instances. Various terms address rebating the funds in case the child doesn't attend a state school, and most of these plans can be transferred easily to a sibling. Many states are limiting these plans now because of concerns that they will be a burden on state coffers.

The second type of 529 plan is one in which the donor of funds (usually parents or relatives) continues to be the owner of the account. These plans allow anyone to give up to a full five years of the allowable tax-free gift allowance all at once. Therefore, a couple could give $110,000 ($11,000 from each parent times five) to a child in a 529 plan at one time without incurring a gift-tax liability. As the donors continue to be the owner of the account until the money is used, the funds can be transferred to another individual as desired. As long as withdrawn funds are used for educational purposes, the earnings on the account are not taxed. Any funds reclaimed by the owner or spent on noneducational costs are taxed (earnings only, not on the original after-tax contribution) and a penalty applied.

These plans are very attractive as an estate planning vehicle for grandparents. The money that is used to fund the account (remember that a grandparent couple could fund $110,000 per child all at once) leaves their estate immediately, yet remains under their control and ownership for potential future needs. Asset protection for money put into 529 plans is undergoing review by state legislatures currently, but the expected trend is that they will not be considered assets of the donor (check with your attorney).

529 plans come in a variety of shapes and sizes. Many are available through no-load fund companies such as Vanguard, Fidelity, and TIAA-CREF. I would highly recommend these choices over those sold by brokers. Most of the plans have asset allocation decisions made by the fund companies, but some newer plans allow some input by the fund owners.

COVERDELL/EDUCATIONAL IRAS

These IRAs allow $2,000 (after-tax) per year to be invested and used for a child's educational needs. The earnings grow and are withdrawn tax-free when used appropriately. A limit to the parents' adjustable gross income prevents most of our clients from directly funding the account. However, the law allows someone other than the parent to fund the account. I'd recommend opening Coverdell accounts for your children and having a relative with a lower gross income fund it yearly. If you choose to reimburse the relative privately, that is your business. Coverdell IRAs can also be used to pay for private secondary school education.

TRADITIONAL AND ROTH IRAS

Withdrawals from IRAs used for educational expenses can be made penalty free, but are subject to a tax on accumulated earnings. This provision precludes withdrawals from a parent's IRA from being a good idea.

However, if you established an IRA for your child from earned income in prior years, this move may work out well. The child is likely to be in a low or even zero tax bracket during college and graduate school years, so this money is never really taxed. It is an excellent idea to employ your children and use $3,000 yearly to fund a traditional IRA (if they earn over $4,850 a year in 2004) and/or a Roth IRA for this purpose. Alternatively, if your child works for someone else, you might help them make IRA contributions. If you don't use the money for education, it makes a nice savings pool for your child's future.

LOANS, GRANTS, TAX CREDITS

If you have significant assets or income, your children will not likely qualify for financial aid. However, most experts recommend filling out the forms in any event, as some schools make "allowances" to enroll students they find desirable for a variety of reasons. It would be worth discussing loan programs with your child's guidance counselor or the school your child plans to attend. An important and often overlooked fact is that your child may be able to claim him- or herself as independent for tax purposes during the college and graduate school years. The child may therefore be able to use HOPE tax credits and Lifetime Learning credits. These are not deductions, but dollar-for-dollar credits applied against any tax liability. Many of our children will have significant assets producing income during their educational years, and these credits may be very useful.

REFERENCES FOR EDUCATIONAL PLANNING

The Best Way to Save for College: A Complete Guide to 529 Plans, 2003–2004 by Joseph F. Hurley. This is the bible of 529 plan information.

www.SavingforCollege.com. An excellent Web site by Joseph F. Hurley (see above listing). It also covers Coverdell IRAs and other college savings ideas.

http://flagship2.vanguard.com/web/planret/Advice PTCollSetSavingsGoal.html. This Vanguard funds site has a college savings calculator, as well as other valuable advice.

www.collegeboard.com. Another great Web site with much useful information on college costs and savings strategies.

www.wiredscholar.com. Yet more excellent online resources to help with your college decision making.

5

Risk Management and Asset Protection

"I haven't been able to sleep well at night since my lawsuit started last year," Jim B. told his wife one night. "I worry about the plaintiff taking away all the savings we have worked so hard to accumulate! I feel too old to make it back up." Jim's wife, not knowing the right thing to say, remained silent.

*P*reservation of what we have worked so hard to accumulate is a major concern for all of us. Malpractice liability is a pressing matter for most physicians; however, we are all increasingly exposed to many other forms of liability. We have business liability, investment liability (in certain cases), and personal injury liability (slip and falls at work or home, teenage drivers, etc.). People who have significant wealth or assets are choice targets as well, thought or known to have deep pockets.

The first tenet of managing exposure to risk is *avoidance*. Usually, this seems to be an issue of common sense, but I have seen some of my peers make themselves very attractive targets for litigation by virtue of aggressive driving and other behaviors. The next consideration in risk management is the *transfer* of at least some of the risk. We buy this risk transfer when we obtain automobile, homeowner's, general liability umbrella, business overhead, health care, malpractice, and virtually every other type of insurance coverage. We are sharing the relatively low chance of a large loss with a number of other people. The important aspect of risk sharing is not to try to share events that are likely to happen and of low cost. For example, a first-dollar or low-deductible insurance policy almost never makes sense. The cost must take into account the high likelihood of making some small claims.

The practical approach is to use high deductibles in almost every type of insurance you purchase. First, ask yourself how large a claim would have to be before you would want or need coverage. For example, I would not want my automobile insurance carrier to know about any claim of less than $1,000, as having the claim on my record might cost more in the long run. If the same is true for you, then raise your automobile insurance deductible to $1,000! A small change in deductible amounts can result in surprisingly large savings.

An additional consideration in risk sharing is how much actual insurance coverage you need. Remember that insurance is really designed to protect you against the *small* chance of a *large* loss. Make sure the large loss is covered. With homeowner's insurance, make sure that your property is insured at an inflation-adjusted replacement value, rather than just a set amount. Make a videotape of your house's internal contents and store it elsewhere. Most homeowner's policies provide only for two-thirds of the outside structure value for internal contents, so if you have valuable objects inside, consider a personal articles policy floater to cover them as well.

ASSET PROTECTION

After methods of risk avoidance and risk sharing are exhausted, or not available, you must consider asset protection. The following discussion is limited in that the author is not an attorney and can only offer general information. You must do the due diligence to learn what the law is where you live.

In Florida, protection from creditors is relatively secure for the following assets:

- Your homestead (your home and a limited amount of property)

- Life insurance and annuities

- IRAs

- Qualified pension plans

- Assets held by husband and wife "as tenants by the entireties"

All of these structures are useful to protect the assets not completely protected by risk sharing or transfer. In many states, owning personal assets jointly titled with a spouse is a common asset protection device. In particular, the titling of assets "As Tenants by the Entireties (ATBE)" in Florida and some other states is still felt to be excellent protection against creditors of a single spouse. This form of ownership implies that each spouse totally owns the asset in question, so that a creditor in a judgment would be violating the property rights of the nontargeted spouse. Ownership as JTROS (jointly held with right of survivorship) might be an acceptable alternative for married couples, but you need to check this with an attorney in your state. Any method of joint ownership in a marriage depends on a continuation of marriage (no death or divorce). Also, creditors of both spouses may still attack assets so titled.

The need for more complex asset protection structures is a function of how much true risk you have, the amount of assets you are trying to protect, and how comfortable you are self-insuring. For example, the use of joint ownership by husband and wife is a very common means of asset protection, but it may not work against the specific risk associated with teenage children drivers. Such a liability could easily extend to joint assets held by husband and wife. For this reason, it is best to add more risk transfer through the purchase of umbrella liability insurance coverage. This coverage picks up where your auto, home, and boat coverage ends. Typically, such insurance is approximately $200 to $300 per $1 million coverage. I recommend no less than $4 million to $5 million of coverage for homes with teenage drivers.

Some of you may feel that you have a higher risk exposure, or that joint ownership by husband and wife is not an answer for you. Single individuals and married couples with shaky marriages do not have the ability to use joint ownership and must calculate their risk assessment accordingly. In these cases and others, more asset protection structures are available to consider.

Family Limited Partnerships

In a family limited partnership (FLP), the assets in question are owned by the general partner (often the parents or a corporation controlled by the parents) and the limited partners (usually the children). An attack by a creditor is usually against a limited partner (as the general partner usually only owns a minimal portion). Allowing the creditor to "take" the limited partner's share is usually considered an unfair attack on the other "innocent" limited partners by partnership law. Therefore, in most cases, a creditor who is successful in obtaining a judgment against a limited partner may only obtain a "charging order," which entitles the creditor to any income distributions due to the limited partner. Because the general partner is a friendly party and determines the amount and timing of such distributions, the creditor usually doesn't receive much and may be induced to settle for a smaller sum. Family limited partnerships also have historically provided some estate planning benefits. Assets so held can be gifted to children utilizing the yearly allowable amounts while the parent/general partner continues to have control of the asset (and much of the generated income). Also, at the time of the gift (at death or before), the limited partnership shares are usually eligible for a "discount" based on the lack of total control of the asset by the limited partner (see the chapter on estate planning).

There are some caveats, however. Utilizing an FLP for asset protection mandates a strict accounting protocol. It is important that the FLP is treated as a separate entity and not as an extension of one's personal assets. Some additional complexity is, therefore, added to our already busy lives, and some additional legal and accounting costs. There have also been some recent court challenges to the asset protection benefits of some FLPs. It would seem prudent to make any such planning for estate rather than strictly asset protection purposes.

Corporate Ownership

Corporate ownership of assets limits the creditor to attacking the assets of the corporation. This ownership is useful in "separating" high-risk assets from your personal holdings. A potential creditor suing you for lia-bility on a corporate-owned property (a rental house or commercial property) can attack only the assets of the corporation, and not your personal holdings. For exam-ple, business real estate (especially rental real estate) is often held in a separate corporate name. A downside to corporate ownership is that your stock in the corpora-tion can be lost in a judgment for the creditor.

Another reason to use a corporate structure is to sep-arate liability from another's actions. If medical or den-tal professionals practice together without a corporate structure, they can theoretically be considered general partners and then each have total unlimited liability for each other. In this corporate setting, the professionals are usually both shareholders and employees of the cor-poration. A malpractice plaintiff has the ability to sue both the individual doctor(s) and the corporation, but cannot attack the personal assets of other noninvolved shareholders.

Limited Liability Company

The limited liability company (LLC) is a very attractive structure for the asset protection of a business or real estate holdings. It is a relatively new legal structure, but has become well understood in most states (check with your lawyer where you live). The LLC provides the asset protection of a corporation, but denies the creditor the ability to obtain ownership. Instead, the judgment creditor is limited to the "charging order" as in a limited partnership. The paperwork of the LLC is simpler and less expensive than setting up a limited partnership, and ongoing documentation is not as onerous.

Equity Stripping

An asset that is highly mortgaged is not attractive to a creditor. In some instances, asset protection can be effected by borrowing against a property and placing the proceeds into a protected structure (life insurance, homestead, offshore, etc.). There is even some opinion that you can use otherwise unprotected cash (during a lawsuit) to pay off a mortgage on your home and not be subject to the charge of a fraudulent conveyance. This method of asset protection is usually considered for investment real estate and increasingly for accounts receivable protection.

Domestic Asset Protection Trusts

Over the last decade, a number of states have established the ability to form trusts that are designed for protection against creditors. These trusts, if set up properly, are written to prevent attack by judgment creditors. There are a number of concerns, however, about their ability to withstand legal challenge. The largest concern is that federal law mandates that each state must honor judgments in another state. Therefore, a judgment against you in your state may be settled by the assets held in one of these other-state domestic asset protection trusts. Many experts warn that these trusts are yet untested by significant creditor attacks.

Offshore Asset Protection Trusts

These trusts involve forming a trust in a selected offshore location. They have provisions that keep you from repatriating the trust assets or their control if you are under legal duress. Done properly, these trusts appear to offer significant asset protection. Done improperly, they have led to jail sentences by judges frustrated at the inability to pull the assets back to the United States. If you are considering this type of asset protection, you must retain an attorney who is highly skilled and experienced in this field. Offshore trust formation is expensive and requires careful documentation and accounting, and it seems most reasonable for a single individual with significant unprotected assets and a high risk of creditor attack.

CONFLICTS BETWEEN ASSET PROTECTION AND ESTATE PLANNING

One goal of estate planning is to preserve the *unified credit*. This credit allows you to leave a certain amount of assets to your heirs without any estate tax liability. Currently this amount is $1.5 million per individual, scheduled to increase gradually to an unlimited amount for 2010 (then revert to a lower amount). Those of us lucky enough to have little to no liability concerns can own enough assets solely to preserve the ability to fund our credit shelter trust. The ownership of assets jointly means that these assets automatically pass to the spouse at death, making them unavailable for funding the "credit shelter trust" that preserves your unified credit. However, in this situation, the credit shelter trust can be funded with pension plan assets (owned solely and protected already), IRAs, and life insurance. On balance, for those of us with asset protection concerns, joint ownership takes precedence over estate planning concerns until we are approaching retirement.

REFERENCES FOR ASSET PROTECTION AND RISK MANAGEMENT

(*COMMENT:* Finding Web sites regarding asset protection that are not proprietary in some sense is almost impossible. Much of the information on these sites is anecdotal and untested. The reading is worthwhile for background, but you must consult a skilled attorney for impartial advice.)

www.FALC.com. Much in the way of interesting reading and opinion.

www.protect-you.com. A strong bias toward offshore trusts, and well done.

www.offshorepress.com. Some of this information is dated, but a comprehensive site otherwise.

Safe Harbors: An Asset Protection Guide for Small Business Owners (CCH Business Owner's Toolkit series) by Nicholas C. Misenti and John L. Duoba (ed.). Less proprietary and more general information than most books on the subject.

6

Health and Disability Planning

"It is terrible about Paul's illness," remarked Jim J. to his colleague Vic over lunch. "I heard he had a huge disability policy and won't have any financial concerns as he fights this thing," answered Vic. Jenkins countered, "I worry about whether or not I have enough, but it is so expensive!"

HEALTH PLANNING

*F*or most of us, health planning means health insurance. As with other types of insurance, what we are really discussing is risk management. We should be attempting to insure primarily against the small risk of a catastrophic loss. However, the health care insurance system is perverse in that it usually is structured to cover even very small claims. For example, we would probably not consider informing our auto insurance carrier about a $250 fender-bender. This is for good reason, as the costs of administering such small claims would in some way be passed back to us in higher premiums. However, we consider our health insurance to be almost first-dollar coverage. We involve the insurance company with paperwork for every medical encounter, no matter how small. The cost of this review and scrutiny is astronomical and certainly contributes significantly to the horrendous rise in health insurance premiums.

Some of you may have little choice in picking your health care coverage. It may come as a benefit of your employer, or you may feel compelled to offer traditional health care insurance for your employees. If you are fortunate enough to choose your own health care coverage, strongly consider a high-deductible policy (at least $2,000 a year per family, and as much as $10,000). Medicare legislation signed into law in late 2003 approved the formation of a Health Savings Account (HSA) for those families with high-deductible policies. You may put away pre-tax money equal to your deductible amount (capped at $5,150 per year) that may be invested and earn interest or capital gains. You may use this HSA to pay for a wide variety of medical and dental expenses (again, all on a pretax basis). You may notify the insurance carrier of your expenses, but they remain uninvolved unless you have a catastrophic illness for which the costs exceed your deductible. My family saved several thousand dollars with such an account last year (then known as a medical savings account). There is usually a discounted prescription plan, but again you pay all the costs of drugs until your deductible is met. You may choose from most providers and hospitals as you are self-insuring, and the latitude in picking providers seems quite large for encounters that exceed your deductible.

To make this coverage more powerful, you may elect to pay for many medical expenses "out of pocket." Now you may leave the HSA full, and let it grow year by year to be available for health care expenses deep into the future.

DISABILITY PLANNING

A significant disability is more likely than a death during your working years. Until or unless you have the assets to self-insure against a prolonged disability, this type of insurance is mandatory.

Several types of disability insurance exist. There is office overhead coverage, short-term disability, and long-term disability. Long-term disability policies are further divided into group and individual coverage types. Finally, Social Security disability must be considered as well.

Short-Term Disability

In the setting of a short-term disability (such as a bad fall on that ski trip), your office expenses continue: rent, employee salaries, and more. It is common and usually not very expensive to have an office overhead policy. These policies usually cover a set amount of office expense for a limited amount of time. Because the coverage is limited, these policies tend to be relatively inexpensive. This coverage is therefore optional for most of us who can self-insure, and rarely necessary for those of us with partners.

Short-term disability policies are also available to replace at least part of your income. They usually begin payment early after a disability and cover you for up to six months. They are typically in place for employees of large corporations, and rarely a good choice for those who can afford to live on savings.

Long-Term Disability

Most long-term disability policies have a waiting period before they begin to pay benefits. Appropriately, a longer wait period results in a cheaper premium. Look at the choices and how much each affects the premium, and determine where you feel you get the best coverage and price. Most of you will find a 90- or 180-day wait period the best fit.

Group disability policies are available, usually through business or professional organizations. These policies are much cheaper than are individual policies (discussed below). They have a "rehab" bent, in that after a certain amount of time they usually restrict their benefits to only more catastrophic disabilities. For example, they may pay benefits for any disability that keeps you from performing your own occupation for two years, but then require you to perform any similar occupation that results in at least 50 percent of prior income after this. A surgeon who lost the use of a hand might lose benefits after two years if he could perform insurance physicals or work in a clinic at half his previous salary. Here is the tradeoff: a cheaper premium for less "individual" coverage. Group long-term disability is usually a great choice for your early years, providing the coverage you need at the lowest possible cost. Another advantage is that premiums don't rise except for the entire "class" of those insured. A downside is that the entire group might be canceled, leaving you uninsured. Although this situation is very rare, it is possible, and could be a real problem if you have developed a new illness since originally purchasing the group policy.

Not as affordable as it once was, individual long-term disability coverage should still be considered. This contract is directly between you and the company only, so it behooves you to choose a company with good financials and staying power. These policies are usually much more friendly to the insured in that they can extend coverage to a disability that is specific to your occupation. For example, you may not be able to perform general dentistry because of a tremor or neck pain, but otherwise be able to function in general day-to-day activities without impairment. A good individual disability policy would pay in this instance. However (as you could guess), these policies are expensive. Find a good agent who specializes in disability insurance and review your options.

Numerous riders on these policies are available. Most waive premiums in the case of disability. Most allow a cost-of-living increase in coverage and premiums. In some instances, these changes require an active choice, so make sure you are clear on this when you purchase the policy. Some allow an increase in coverage without a new medical re-evaluation, a very valuable right in the case of acquired illness. As with other insurance, follow the principle of insuring against the catastrophic loss when choosing disability coverage.

The Social Security Administration provides disability coverage as well. The qualifications are quite strict and rigid, being "the inability to perform any occupation." A catastrophic illness is necessary to trigger this coverage, and the benefits are limited to about $15,000 to $30,000 each year. However, if you remain disabled, you will receive Medicare coverage automatically after two years. This combination of disability payments and Medicare insurance coverage should be built into your disability insurance evaluation.

Another issue to consider is just how much coverage you need, which is a highly individual determination. There are formulas that relate to your income level, but these assume that you spend all your current income. Determine what your yearly cost of living is likely to be and purchase this coverage (less your ability to self-insure from savings). Some costs of your lifestyle might change significantly (higher or lower) in the event of a disability.

Also consider whether the benefits of the policy will be taxable or not. If the disability premiums are paid as a tax-deductible expense of your business, then the premiums are taxable. If you pay the premiums with after-tax money, the benefits are tax free. Plan accordingly.

LONG-TERM CARE INSURANCE

Disability-related loss of income is also usually combined with attendant health care costs. It is not unusual for the illness or accident that results in a given disability to also result in the need for care such as home health support or rehab/nursing home care. The cost of such care has skyrocketed. A nursing home stay can easily cost between $40,000 and $100,000 per year. Accordingly, insurance carriers have begun to offer coverage designed to cover these costs, but there is a great deal of variability on what is covered and for how long. There are qualified long-term care insurance policies that meet government guidelines, and their premiums are tax deductible. If you are considering such a policy, seek an expert in the field.

By the time most of us start thinking about the need for long-term care insurance, we should have saved enough to self-insure against these needs. This is a very individual decision that involves your penchant for risk taking, your attitude towards premium costs, and your level of savings.

REFERENCES FOR HEALTH AND DISABILITY PLANNING

http://consumerlawpage.com/article/insure.shtml. A variety of articles on long-term care insurance.

www.longtermcarelink.net/#useful_links. Another source of articles to begin your research.

www.healthinsuranceinfo.net. A nonprofit site for health insurance issues.

www.about-disability-insurance.com.
This proprietary site run by an agent links to a lot of good articles and terms.

Nolo's Guide to Social Security Disability: Getting & Keeping Your Benefits (Nolo's Guide to Social Security Disability, 2nd ed.) by David A. Morton III, MD.

www.pueblo.gsa.gov/results.tpl?id1=16&startat=1&--woSECTIONSdatarq=16&--SECTIONSword=ww. Federal guides to consumer information on health, disability, and LTC insurance.

7

Life Insurance and Annuities

"I fended off yet another life insurance salesman on the phone today," Jim B. told his wife over dinner. "Do we have enough life insurance with the baby coming?" she asked. His perturbed look answered her question.

*T*he very topic of life insurance stirs up a hornet's nest of responses both from clients and other advisors. To clients, it is a warning of mortality. To advisors, it is a source of friction on whether it is an investment, protection, or sometimes just a rip-off of their clients.

The monetary arguments about life insurance are related to whether the coverage should be term or cash value. Term insurance is just that: protection purchased for a certain period of time. It is clearly the cheapest form of life insurance, offering the benefit of most coverage (face value or death benefit) for least premium outlay. It has no savings component and becomes more expensive every year (as your risk of dying increases). You may, however, buy multiple-year level term insurance in which this yearly increase is built into a level premium for a longer term. It is not usually guaranteed for life and must be renewed with a physical exam every so many years (which may prove troublesome if you develop a serious illness in the interim). Insurance agents don't make much money on selling this insurance, and therefore tend to push the more rewarding (for them) cash value or permanent insurance. They make an argument that most term insurance lapses before it ever pays a death benefit. However, this is not necessarily a negative, as term insurance is specifically designed to cover just those periods of time in which you feel that insurance is important.

You can buy term insurance through an insurance agent, but in this day and age the Internet has become valuable in this regard. Term insurance is somewhat of a commodity product, with the important features being:

- Quality of the company. Will it be there to pay your heirs?

- Length of term guaranteed if a certain premium is paid.

- Guaranteed renewability with or without a physical exam.

- Convertibility to cash value insurance if so desired.

- Cost of the premiums.

Most of these features can now be compared on the Internet using sites noted in the references at the end of the chapter.

Cash value life insurance is a totally different and complex product. Think of your cash value premiums as being divided into three separate accounts, paying for

- The equivalent cost of term insurance based on your age and health.

- The "overhead" of the insurance company.

- The savings component.

ARGUMENTS FOR CASH VALUE INSURANCE

The special tax treatment of the savings component makes cash value life insurance so confusing, but also worth considering. Money in the savings component grows tax-free unless the policy is canceled. At some point the policy will probably throw off enough income to pay your premiums internally (no more external premium payments), essentially using tax-free income for that purpose.

The savings component can be invested several different ways. It can receive a fixed amount of interest (like a CD) or be invested in mutual funds (called variable insurance). You may "borrow" the savings component by taking policy loans. Your initial loans are considered a return of the premiums you paid in (despite the fact that they were used partially to purchase the term component of the insurance and pay expenses). The next amount loaned is the build-up in earnings and the contributions to the savings component. Because the insurance company is in essence lending you your own money, the cost of these loans (interest rate) is very low, sometimes zero. Despite the fact that you are withdrawing earnings that have never been taxed, you may spend these loans and never pay tax on them, as long as you keep your policy in force. If you die with loans outstanding, the amount is deducted from your death benefit. This combination of tax-free growth and use of the funds, along with the strong asset protection offered by life insurance, makes it a compelling choice for many.

ARGUMENTS AGAINST
CASH VALUE INSURANCE

There are a few good arguments against buying cash value insurance.

First, many people argue that individuals who buy life insurance in the early part of their careers need a higher death benefit than they can afford with cash value insurance. Accordingly, they should buy term instead. I think this argument is valid, and your insurance purchase should always consider need for the death benefit first (see discussion below on how much insurance to purchase). This does not preclude replacing or adding to your term coverage with cash value insurance later on when you can afford it.

Second, many argue that the commissions paid to life insurance agents (often as much as 100 percent of the first year's premium) make it a bad investment. A compelling argument is that the early loss of so much of the savings component makes it hard to catch up in later years. At times you need the advice of a good agent, who earns a commission for his or her work. However, some new policies spread out the cost of the commission over later years, allowing you to build cash value faster. In addition, I strongly recommend you review no-load/low-load life insurance. One such company is Ameritas Direct, which is easy to work with on the phone. There are a few other highly rated companies now offering such policies by phone, Internet, and mail. They are a small percentage of the market, because insurance is typically sold and not bought. There are also fee-only insurance planners who specialize in life insurance policies and can presumably give you impartial advice on complex issues for an agreed-upon and reasonable fee.

A third argument is made that you must keep cash value life insurance in place until death to avoid paying tax on all the internal build-up of earnings. Many of us don't need life insurance at death if we have significant assets, but many of us purchase life insurance for estate planning reasons. The cost of continuing the coverage late in life can be mitigated by having the cash value/savings component act as part or all of the death benefit. Depending on how many policy loans you have taken, you may actually have accumulated a savings component that is similar to the size of the death benefit. In this case, most policies allow you to fund the death benefit with your own money, greatly reducing the need to buy internal coverage.

A final argument is that the government may change the way in which insurance is treated. It may decide to means-test the ability to take policy loans or tax the internal build-up. Although this is possible, past attempts to tax insurance benefits have failed. In addition, if you do use a no-load policy, you can collapse the policy if the law changes. Your net cost is not too much different than if you had bought term and invested the difference.

A variant of cash-value insurance is known as universal life coverage. This product allows changing premiums and death benefits based on insurability. With this insurance, there is a marked transparency of the three expense components (term insurance cost, expenses, and overhead). You also are allowed more flexibility on how much premium you wish to pay each month (allowing you to vary the savings contribution). If you are disciplined, this is a good choice of cash value insurance to consider.

HOW MUCH LIFE INSURANCE DO YOU NEED?

This question is as complex as asking how much money you need to live. Several methods of making this calculation are available. In the *income replacement model*, a lump sum that would replace the stream of income from your earnings is purchased as a death benefit. It does not necessarily adjust for the fact that you won't be in the picture to spend some of that money. In the *calculation of needs* method, an advisor makes a best guess of the particular circumstances of your heirs in terms of their income needs for future years. Then, a current lump-sum amount is calculated that would provide this stream of income (again with assumptions on investment returns and inflation). Every method is somewhat crude, but you have to start somewhere. Every individual is different, as is every heir.

In a couple of instances life insurance may not be necessary. If you have sufficient assets to provide for your heirs, then you have no absolute need for life insurance. If you don't have heirs who need support, then you don't need life insurance (the single individual with no dependents). However, in this case it may still be prudent to obtain some insurance in case a significant illness develops in the interim, reducing or proscribing coverage when it is needed.

ANNUITIES

Annuities involve giving money to an insurance company in exchange for a promise to pay you back in some fashion in the future. With a deferred annuity, the insurance company invests the money you give them and promises to pay you a lump sum or stream of income in the future. The savings component is the funds you initially deposit. Just as with life insurance, this savings account can receive a fixed income or be invested in mutual funds (a variable annuity). Like variable life insurance, a variable annuity puts the risk of the savings component with the buyer, in exchange for a potentially higher return. One salient point and an advantage of variable annuities is that the insurance company usually guarantees that you will be able to annuitize *(see below)* no less than your original deposit, even if your investment experience is lousy.

You "annuitize" when you decide to begin receiving an income stream. This is immediately with an immediate annuity, and with a time of your choosing (after age 59½, however, to draw income without a penalty) with a deferred annuity. The income is partly a return of your original deposit and partially earnings on the deposit. The earnings component is taxed at ordinary income rates regardless of how long you had the annuity.

Because of the ordinary income tax rates assessed on earnings, as well as usually high costs of annuity products, many advisors have frowned upon their use in the past. However, there are some very good reasons to consider them as part of your portfolio. There are now high-quality, no-load, low-expense annuities available through fund companies like Vanguard, TIAA-CREF, and Fidelity Funds. In addition, annuities offer instant asset protection. Finally, many advisors now are beginning to appreciate the security of having some of one's assets in an annuity during retirement. Much of what advisors do in retirement planning is try to ensure that you have enough money to live on without anxiety. An annuity does just that, in that it is usually structured to make payments based on your and your spouse's life expectancy. A downside is that the amount you receive isn't adjusted for inflation, so that many advisors are now considering having clients use annuities only late in life.

When you do annuitize, you have several choices on how to receive the income stream. One choice that produces the highest income flow is to receive payments until your death. If you die early, the insurance company does well, and vice versa. You can choose several other options, all of which pay less (per month). Many people choose to have payments continue until both husband and wife are dead. You may also choose a "term certain" policy that pays a fixed number of years rather than a term based on a lifetime.

REFERENCES FOR LIFE INSURANCE AND ANNUITIES

www.nolo.com. Several brief useful articles on choosing life insurance.

www.AmeritasDirect.com. A proprietary site for no-load and low-load life insurance and annuities.

www.Vanguard.com. A source for no-load, low expense annuities.

www.feeplannersnetwork.com. A place to find fee-only insurance agents and planners.

www.insurancecalculators.com/needscalc.htm. One of many life insurance calculators on the Internet. This one uses the income replacement method.

8

Charitable Planning

"I'd like to teach my kids to be charitable, and to learn about how unfortunate some others' lives can be," Jim P. told his financial advisor. "You have been very fortunate, and our investing style has done well. You should consider setting up a private charitable foundation at the time of your death, and have your children employed on the board that must research the choices for contributions by the foundation," the advisor replied.

merica is an altruistic country. Our level of charitable giving is unmatched throughout the world. Our clients commonly consider charitable causes as they realize that they have reached a point of financial security. Sometimes there is an attachment to a particular charity or cause, but others remain generally disposed to help others.

You need to consider a number of things when deciding to give money to a charitable cause. Done correctly, your contributions can go further and be of a larger value without an increase in out-of-pocket costs to you. Charitable planning can be a complex topic with severe tax penalties if not done correctly, and I'd advise expert help by a tax attorney in any decision involving a significant amount of money.

OUTRIGHT GIFTS

Gifting is certainly the easiest and most common way to be charitable. It is a completely irrevocable way to give money away, which means it can't be taken back. You should know that the government actually puts limits on how much you can give away without paying a tax, and on what form the gift might take.

For example, if you gift away more than $11,000 to an individual in a given year, you must file a gift tax return. The amount greater than $11,000 will actually be deducted from your ability to leave money tax free from your estate (the unified credit). In addition, if you have gift tax liabilities of over $1 million during life, you must actually pay a significant tax on the amount gifted. This law is in place to prevent wealthier people from gifting away most of their assets late in life to avoid an estate tax. There is no limit on the amount you leave directly to a charitable organization, or pay directly to an educational or medical institution on someone else's behalf. It is useful to remember these ways to gift to others without triggering gift tax consequences.

Gifts to a charitable institution have complexities as well. There are actual limits to how much you may gift per year to charity, based on your income level. The type of gift (cash or not) also triggers somewhat complex regulations on what is an allowable and deductible gift, often based your adjusted gross income. As an example, a gift of art to an institution that is not in the business of art (say, the Boy Scouts) is valued at the cost of the materials regardless of the value of the painting. However, the same painting given to a museum is valued at its market worth. Consult an accountant or tax attorney regarding gifts of significant amounts.

You may combine your ability to give the $11,000 per individual per year with your spouse, so that a couple could give $22,000 per year to an individual without any tax consequences. For example, a set of grandparents could gift up to $110,000 per year to a family of five (related or not). An exception to this limit is found with Educational 529 plans in which a full five years of deductions can be taken all at once. So, a couple could gift $110,000 to one person in a given year, with the expectation that the gift is to be used for educational purposes only.

A relatively new way to make outright gifts is with Donor Advised Funds. Vanguard and Fidelity Funds are two companies with such funds. You may donate cash or appreciated stock to these funds, and the money is invested in mutual funds that you choose. Your charitable gift deduction is taken in full in the year(s) in which you make the gift to the fund. At any time in the future, you instruct the fund to donate some of your account to charitable institutions. If your gift grows with the investments you choose, so much the better for the charities that benefit.

Be aware that charitable gifts are considered Schedule A deductions (along with real estate taxes and mortgage interest) on your tax return. The IRS disallows approximately $3,000 of Schedule A deductions for every $100,000 of adjusted gross income over approximately $140,000. If you are fortunate enough to not have mortgage interest, your charitable contributions may have up to 80 percent of the amount you give disallowed in some cases. Talk to your accountant about this.

Gifting may occur at the time of your death (testamentary gifts). Such gifting results in a decrease in estate taxes. Another type of gifting involves the purchase of life insurance with a charity being the beneficiary. These transactions and the gifts of existing life insurance policies to individuals are governed by complex tax law and should be reviewed carefully.

CHARITABLE TRUSTS AND ANNUITIES

This type of charitable giving is common with high-net-worth individuals (hopefully the readers of this book). The IRS allows a partial tax deduction of these limited gifts. In the case of the charitable remainder annuity trust (CRAT), something of value (land, money, stock, etc.) is given to a charitable organization in exchange for an income from the charity for an agreed-upon term. The charity is able to sell appreciated property or stock and invest the entire untaxed amount of money so gained in order to pay the income to the donor. The donor also receives an immediate tax deduction based on IRS tables, and then the income as agreed upon. The terms of this income are quite negotiable with various charities, usually related to the ages of the donors and the prevailing rates of investment interest. A CRAT may result in a significant return on one's gift as well as a substantial charitable donation with only the government tax coffers paying the price.

A common suggested method of structuring one's affairs late in life in order to benefit both your charities and your heirs involves using a CRAT and an irrevocable life insurance trust (ILIT). There is more to read on ILITs in the chapter on estate planning. Suffice it to say that these trusts are set up as independent entities to hold insurance on your life, with your heirs as the beneficiaries. You give appreciated property or cash to the CRAT. You receive an up-front tax deduction as well as an income stream. Using your tax savings, and as much of the income stream as you wish, you gift money to the ILIT to pay for the premiums on the life insurance contained within. When you die, the life insurance funds the trust both estate and income tax–free, and your heirs have "replaced" the value of the property left to the charity, at little or no net cost to you. Everybody benefits except the IRS.

There is also the charitable lead trust (CLAT) to consider. In this case, the donor gives the charity the income from a donation. At the end of the trust term, the remaining funds go to heirs (or even the donor) with little or no tax due. There is an upfront tax deduction based on the terms of the trust, and the net effect is designed to pass appreciating assets on to heirs with no estate or gift taxes.

There are also regular charitable annuities, in which a donation to a charitable fund offers a guaranteed return of an income stream until death or for a certain term. This again is a way to take some money that would have gone to pay estate or income taxes and benefit a charity, while preserving much of your net after-tax income from the donation.

Finally, you may fund a personal foundation to carry on charitable activities. These entities are usually created by an individual family and are used to have continued control and direction in the disposition of charitable assets over time. In the case of multimillion-dollar foundations, family members are often included to help manage the foundation. This allows a source of income to heirs, as well as some continuity of purpose in forming the foundation. Seek expert counsel on this, but most experts feel that the complexity and expense of forming and running a foundation requires at least a million-dollar contribution.

REFERENCES FOR CHARITABLE GIVING

Most charitable organizations can give you a wealth of information on gifting programs and charitable trusts.

www.give.org. A site to check out your charitable organization for efficiency and track record.

www.charitablegift.org. Fidelity Funds Donor Advised Fund. Much information is present here, and the fund is very similar to other funds' programs.

PricewaterhouseCoopers' Guide to Charitable Giving, by PricewaterhouseCoopers; Michael B. Kennedy, Evelyn M. Capassakis, and Richard S. Wagman. A good general guide to various ways to help others.

9

Estate Planning

Alex Johnson, CFP, walked into his office and spoke to his partner, Sally. "I just had to explain to another client that a living trust would not save them any estate taxes. There is so much misinformation out there!"

GENERAL PRINCIPLES OF
ESTATE PLANNING

*T*here are two primary purposes of estate planning. First, a major purpose is to direct the disposition of one's assets (and guardianship of children if an issue). The second purpose is to minimize the taxes applied to property at the time of death.

The standard will is adequate to direct the disposition of estate property, but the use of trusts allows more control and flexibility. A trust is a legal entity that allows a trustee to control assets (the trust corpus) for the benefit of a beneficiary. A trust formed at the time of death is termed a *testamentary trust* and is irrevocable at that time by virtue of the grantor (the forming party of the trust) being dead. Most of our wills direct that property not otherwise designated "pour over" into a trust(s).

Some of us also have living trusts. These are revocable, meaning that the property can be directed during life and reclaimed by the grantor or his/her creditors. Living trusts therefore do not provide any tax or estate savings, but do offer a rapid change in control at the time of death without the need for probate. A living trust may also be funded at death by the will (again, by a "pour over provision" and serve as the testamentary trust also.

At the time of death, any solely owned property not titled in a way that allows someone else to immediately own or control it (jointly held assets and assets in a living trust) will pass through a probate system. The probate court determines how the said property is to pass, based on wills and state law. In the overwhelming majority of cases, this is not the headache we read about, but a formality that takes several months. However, most estate planners have their clients' assets owned jointly or in a living trust so that probate is a minor concern.

TRUSTS

Trusts allow the grantor (the person forming the trust) to direct that assets in the trust be controlled by a trustee of his/her choice. The trustee manages and disburses these assets for beneficiaries of the trust (usually the spouse and children, but can be anyone or an organization). The use of trusts *(see below)* allows some estate tax savings and also some very specific control over how the assets can be distributed.

Understand that only a few ways are available to leave assets at the time of your death that do not subject the assets to immediate estate taxation. First, you can fund the "bypass trust" with the legally maximal excludable amount *(see below)*. Second, you may leave an unlimited amount of assets to your spouse without any estate tax liability. Third, you may leave assets to charity without any tax liability on this amount. A fourth way is to never really "own" the asset in question. For example, assets owned by an irrevocable trust *(see below)* that pass at your death were not technically owned by you. Also life insurance proceeds to beneficiaries are not "owned" by you and pass estate tax–free—unless the beneficiary is your own estate.

Generally, most estate planners use two trusts in their documents. The first is known as the bypass or credit shelter trust. This trust is funded (usually) with the amount of money that the government allows each individual to leave estate tax–free ($1.5 million in 2004). In most instances, the trustee of the bypass trust is the spouse, and the assets therein are for his/her benefit with the children as the secondary beneficiaries. If you look at a credit shelter trust, you will usually notice some unusual wording, specifying that the trustee may distribute money from the trust for the maintenance, education, support, and health of the beneficiaries, which means that the trust cannot distribute money for just any reason. These limits (which in reality are very loose—as what exactly is "support" and what is "maintenance"?) are called *ascertainable standards*, and by IRS law allow the trust to avoid being considered under the total control and ownership of the trustee/spouse. Therefore, when the spouse dies, the trust assets continue to pass on to secondary beneficiaries without tax being due. If instead, the trustee/spouse has total control of the trust (*general powers of appointment*), then the trust assets would be taxed at death, and in fact the money would have never really escaped estate taxation.

Use of the credit shelter/bypass trust allows each couple to leave $3 million tax free (in 2004) to their heirs. A standard basis of estate tax planning is to "fund" the maximal amount allowed for each spouse or individual. This approach can come into conflict with asset protection issues, as joint ownership used for asset protection may preclude the ability to fund bypass trusts. Most often, the bypass trust is then funded by life insurance proceeds or pension plan assets (never technically jointly owned). You may wish to review your life insurance and pension plan beneficiary designations for this reason with an estate planning attorney.

The second trust most of us have formed at our deaths is the marital trust, which is a way of saying that all the assets not left to the credit shelter trust are left in trust to the spouse. The spouse is usually the trustee and does not have limits on distributions of income and principal, as the assets in this trust will be taxed in the spouse's estate in any event. This trust is not essential, as any assets left in the will to the spouse not in a trust are treated the same way. Some clients like the idea of a trust to help the spouse avoid future creditors (with a spendthrift provision that prevents the creditors from attaching trust assets), or for other reasons of control. There are also so-called QTIP trusts used to control the assets left to a spouse in a way to ensure that children from a previous marriage ultimately receive some of the trust assets.

The complex issue of how assets can be left to grandchildren and the related tax issues won't be discussed here. You may see reference in estate tax documents to generation-skipping trusts or GST amounts. This refers to the taxation of assets to those more than a generation away from you. If you wish or plan to leave significant sums to grandchildren, you should seek expert advice.

GIFTING

Another common idea in estate tax planning is to reduce your estate through the use of gifts during life. Any such gift is removed from your estate immediately. The IRS, however, seeks to prevent the use of large gifts as a means of escaping estate taxation, so you need to understand the rules on this topic.

You may only leave $11,000 per person per year without incurring gift tax liability. Therefore, a couple may leave $22,000 per year to anyone and everyone they wish without any gift tax liability. If you have three children, you and your spouse can gift away $66,000 per year that will then be removed from your estate. Most people try to stay inside the $11,000 per-year, per-person allowances, as there is no limit to these gifts. There is also the ability to leave untaxed gifts under several circumstances. For example, money given directly to an educational or medical institution for the benefit of someone else is not considered a taxable gift.

If your estate is substantial, this amount of gifting may be inadequate. In a lifetime, you can gift up to $1 million (over and above amounts that escape gift tax liability) without actually paying a tax. Gifts over $1 million carry the responsibility of an immediate gift tax payment. It is not quite that simple, but it is usually enough to understand these limits and exclusions. Beginning in 2004, there is a difference in the amount that can be gifted without tax and the amount that can be excluded from the estate tax. Consult your attorney or planner.

FAMILY LIMITED PARTNERSHIPS

These entities are also discussed in the chapter on asset protection, as they offer the triple benefits of protecting your assets, reducing estate taxes, and also lowering your income tax burden in some cases. Many families place property into FLPs for all or some of these reasons. Typically, parents form the FLP with themselves or a corporation as the general partner (retaining control), but owning only about 1 percent of the entire entity. They are also the limited partners, owing the other 99 percent in this capacity. An attack by creditors allows the defense of charging orders (see the chapter on asset protection). The parents may gift away parts of the limited partnership interest with a discount. For example, a percentage of the FLP worth $20,000 would be considered to be worth only $11,000 in some cases, as the FLP interest comes with no control or marketability. In this fashion, the parents' assets may be disbursed in a more rapid fashion, while they remain in control. The parents might even keep most of the income from the FLP, paying themselves a management fee rather than distributing income to the limited partners. However, the third benefit of the FLP is that if the parents do distribute income to the children by virtue of their FLP interest, the children will probably pay income tax in a lower bracket.

PRIVATE ANNUITIES

This is a method of transferring assets out of the parents' estate while protecting their cash flow. In a typical arrangement, the parents transfer an asset to the children, who then agree to pay regular mortgage-like payments until one or both parents die. The value of the payments must meet IRS calculations equal to the present value of the asset. When the parent(s) die, the annuity payments stop. One problem with this structure is that if the parents live much longer than expected, then the children have a higher cost for the asset than anticipated. This situation is mitigated somewhat by the fact that the asset transfer doesn't trigger the horrendous estate tax.

A variant of the personal annuity is the Qualified Personal Residence Trust. In this case the parents' home is transferred to the children in a trust that allows the parents to remain for a specified number of years.

The value of the home is a gift, but reduced by a value imputed to the right for the parents to live there for a number of years. At the end of the term, the home becomes the property of the children, who may then lease it to the parents. This plan effects the transfer of a valuable home at a reduced valuation.

IRREVOCABLE LIFE INSURANCE TRUSTS

A common method of using a trust to avoid estate taxes is to fund an irrevocable life insurance trust (ILIT). These trusts are set up as independent entities to hold insurance on your life, with your heirs as the beneficiaries. You may gift the cost of the life insurance premiums to the trust (within limits). If you give the beneficiaries a limited right to "withdraw" the gifted amount each year (so called Crummey powers), then the gift is considered a "present value gift," and therefore allowable as a nontaxable event (up to $11,000 per beneficiary per year). The money for the yearly gift to the ILIT might be directly from your assets or from the income stream from a CRAT (see the section on charitable giving). When you die, the life insurance funds the trust, both estate- and income-tax free. Estate taxes are avoided by the virtue of the fact that you never really owned or controlled the trust or the life insurance inside it.

529 PLANS

An interesting and new twist in allowable gifts occurs in State 529 Educational Plans. These plans allow anyone to gift five full years of the allowable limit of money in one year. Therefore a couple could give $110,000 at once ($11,000 from each parent, times five) to a child in a 529 plan without incurring a gift tax liability. These plans are even more interesting as the assets continue to be owned by the donors until used by the beneficiary. However, the money is considered out of the estate at the time of the gift, despite this continuation of control. The owners may change beneficiaries as needed or desired, or may use the money themselves (although this will trigger a tax and penalty on the earnings). This is discussed in more detail in the chapter on educational planning.

ADDITIONAL ESTATE PLANNING

A good estate plan should include the execution of durable power of attorney forms, living will forms, and health care surrogate forms. This latter form allows someone whom you trust to make medical decisions for you in the event of severe illness or other incapacity. The durable power of attorney allows someone to make legal and financial decisions for you in the same circumstances.

REFERENCES FOR ESTATE PLANNING

Tools and Techniques of Estate Planning, 12th edition, by Steve Leimberg. Regularly updated, this series is written for financial advisors. However, it is eminently readable for those with a strong interest in the topic.

Estate Planning for Dummies, by Jordan Simon and Brian Caverly. Surprisingly well done, as are most of the "Dummies" series I've read.

www.estateplanninglinks.com/. A proprietary site with great links.

www.nolo.com. Nolo is a good site for books, software, and articles on a number of legal and financial topics.

10

Tax Planning

Dr. Kevin L. complained to his accountant, "I feel that I'm working endless hours and the government is taking half of my income away. Surely there are some tricks you can use to help me keep more of my hard-earned money?"

Over the last two decades, there has been a trend toward a reduction in marginal tax rates. Unfortunately, this change has been accompanied by a similar reduction in the ability to make tax deductions. Although this has helped us all avoid extreme measures to save on taxes, it has also resulted in a generally higher tax burden for upper-income taxpayers. At the current time, the government has given us a new break on capital gains taxes and on taxation of dividends from stocks.

INCOME

Income from almost any source (other than tax-free municipal bonds) and from anywhere (including over-seas accounts) is subject to taxation in the United States. All of your practice or business income is considered ordinary income, which is taxable at the highest current legal rates. Most of the readers of this book probably pay income tax in the highest bracket (currently 35 percent). This means that every additional dollar you make or earn on some investments is taxed at 35 percent. Wage income is also subject to a 1.5–3 percent Medicare tax, but income from investments is not.

Interest income is also taxable as ordinary income. Income from bonds and bond funds is considered interest income despite being called dividends (in the case of bond funds). However, dividends paid on common stocks (held at least sixty days) are now taxed at a maximum rate of 15 percent.

Capital gains (or losses) are the profit or loss realized when you own something and sell it—whether it's real estate, tangible items such as art or jewelry, or most common stocks and bonds. Something owned for more than one year results in a long-term capital gain or loss, and a shorter time of ownership results in a short-term capital gain or loss. New tax law in 2003 reduced long-term capital gains rates to only 15 percent, but mostly only on stock and bond investments. Collectibles and real estate transactions retain higher rates (although the sale of your primary residence allows a gain of up to $500,000 before taxes are assessed).

Income that comes out of IRAs, qualified retirement plans, and annuities (excluding return of contributed principal) is all taxed at ordinary income rates. The new lower rates on stock dividends and long-term capital gains have led some advisors to rethink the idea of fully funding retirement plans. Other advisors favor a continuation of funding any vehicle that allows long-term compounding in a tax-deferred manner.

DEDUCTIONS

The first area of allowable deductions on your taxes is the exemptions for you and your dependents, although these are phased out at higher income levels. Second, there are allowed deductions for student loan interest, health insurance, and HSA contributions (see health and disability planning for HSA information), alimony paid, moving expenses, contributions to retirement plans, and one half of any self-employment taxes you paid. The resulting amount is your adjusted gross income (AGI). From your AGI, you may take a standard deduction (again, partially or totally eliminated for high-income taxpayers) or you may itemize deductions. To itemize entails filling out Schedule A with deductions for the several categories. Medical expenses that exceed 7.5 percent of your AGI are deductible. You may also deduct state and local taxes, real estate taxes, and interest paid on your mortgages (within limits). Investment interest is deductible up to the limits of your investment income. Charitable gifts (cash and property) are deductible, as are miscellaneous expenses such as tax preparation fees and investment advisory costs (as they exceed 2 percent of your AGI).

An important point to note is that you lose the ability to deduct $3,000 of your Schedule A deductions for every $100,000 your AGI exceeds $137,500. There is a partial exclusion of this loss for charitable donations. Simple, isn't it? The point to note is that if you have an AGI of $400,000 a year, you lose the ability to deduct almost $10,000 of your Schedule A amount. Those of you who do not make mortgage payments will therefore lose the ability to deduct some of your charitable and real estate tax payments. In this case, it pays to bunch your Schedule A deductions on an every-other-year basis, which can then save thousands of dollars in tax payments. For example, if you have $20,000 a year in charitable donations and real estate taxes and also have an AGI of $437,500, you would lose the ability to deduct approximately $9,000. If you instead bunch these payments, then you would have a $40,000 deduction every other year. You would still lose $9,000 in deductions, but only every other year, rather than yearly. This produces a net savings of $4,500 per year using a simple maneuver.

TAX SHELTERS

There are still programs offering tax credits for low-income housing and oil/gas drilling. A credit is different from a deduction, in that a dollar of a credit lowers your tax by a dollar, but a dollar of a deduction lowers your tax by the percentage of tax you pay (usually thirty-five cents). These investments are usually loaded with fees and risk and very long-term commitments of capital. They deserve more scrutiny than consideration.

TAX PLANNING

There are a few ways that you might lower your tax burden in the current environment. Consider the following suggestions and see what fits your particular situation:

- When possible, try to hold your investments for more than a year in order to qualify for the very low 15 percent long-term capital gains tax rate.

- Consider obtaining income from stock dividends with their new low tax rate of 15 percent.

- Fully fund your retirement plans. This contribution escapes immediate taxation and is allowed to grow tax-free until withdrawal much later on. Despite the argument that it may convert possible long-term capital gains and dividends taxed at 15 percent to ordinary income taxed at a higher ordinary income bracket in the future, it still makes sense. Pretax retirement plan contributions trade three taxes for the sole ordinary income taxation at withdrawal. They postpone immediate ordinary income tax on the income contributed up front. They avoid ongoing yearly capital gains from sales and ordinary income tax on interest. Finally, they avoid capital gains tax on final sales from your savings. Also, who knows how we'll be taxed in the future?

• You can income shift to children in several ways. The first $750 in unearned income (interest and dividends) owned by a child (UTMA accounts) is untaxed, and the next $750 is taxed very lightly. After age fourteen, the child may pay taxes in his/her own tax bracket (usually low). Also each child may earn $4,850 per year (at any age) without an income tax being due. Consider paying your children (with jobs that are age appropriate) for work in your business. You get a deduction (35 percent taxable money otherwise), and the kids get tax-free income (up to $4,850 per year). If you are a sole proprietor, then there are no Social Security taxes due either. Strongly consider a Roth IRA for $3,000 of the child's earnings. Even better, the child can earn another $3,000 per year ($7,850), and fund a fully deductible traditional IRA. Still no tax due, and you have saved a bundle.

- If you are not subject to a high risk of liability, consider employing your spouse. Not only is the salary deductible, but your spouse may make significant retirement plan contributions as well.

- If you are over age fifty and have few employees, investigate a defined benefit retirement plan, which may allow deductions much higher than the $40,000-per-year limit on defined contribution plans (see the chapter on retirement planning).

- Whenever possible, take the deduction at the corporate level. Small corporations are less likely to be investigated by the IRS, and your personal return will be that much "cleaner."

CREDITS

After you have taken all your allowable deductions, you have arrived at the tax owed. From this amount you are possibly able to apply tax credits. As discussed above, tax credits allow a dollar-for-dollar reduction in the tax owed, whereas a deductible dollar only saves you about thirty-five cents in the tax owed. The possible tax credits include foreign tax paid (on foreign investments) and a variety of credits for child care and some educational expenses. However, most of these credits only apply to low-income taxpayers.

Your final tax due is the difference between what you owe and have already paid in withholding and estimated tax payments. Pay it, and focus on adding to and growing your saved assets.

REFERENCES FOR TAX PLANNING

www.TurboTax.com. A proprietary site with much good information.

www.IRS.gov. The motherlode!

www.1040.com. Another proprietary site with much good information and many links.

11

Working with Advisors

"I'm furious at my investment performance with the new broker I switched to last year," exclaimed Susan J. to her partner, Janet. "What's worse, I was told that I have to pay surrender charges if I want to sell the funds he bought, despite the fact they have underperformed in nearly every case."

FINANCIAL PLANNERS
AND ADVISORS

*I*am clearly biased towards fee-only financial advice. In fact, the overwhelming majority of "advisors" you encounter are paid (at least in part) by virtue of product sales, and not on the basis of fees. Even many brokerage-associated advisors who charge you a wrap fee are motivated internally by their employers to sell certain funds and insurance products. These advisors serve two masters: you and the one who cuts their paycheck. This is not to say that ethical advice is limited to fee-only advisors, but choosing one shifts the odds in your favor. The fee-only advisor's interests are aligned with yours, and his/her only occupation is to give you advice. Be careful of the term "fee-based," as this implies that the advisor can make money with fees or commissions. You can find a fee-only planner at *www.fpanet.org* or *www.Napfa.org*.

ACCOUNTANTS

You need an accountant. Despite the lure of computerized tax software, you really can't do it yourself. Your accountant should be a C.P.A. (certified public accountant), which ensures a high level of education in most aspects of tax planning. If you do not have a C.P.A., ask your peers for their recommendations or interview some candidates. Most likely, you will stay with an accountant for many years, and you should have a mutually beneficial relationship.

In past years, some accountants seemed much more open toward tax minimization than did others. The IRS monitors accountants for "aggressive" practices and can potentially subject the clients of certain accountants to an increased percentage of audits. Most accountants have you sign a waiver of responsibility as well, documenting that the information they put down is from you directly. It pays to keep up with tax savings ideas and to run them by your financial planner as well as your accountant on a regular basis.

One caution is accountants who have a "sales" side. A small percentage of accountants in the country have earned the P.F.S. designation. If they are fee-only planners, you should consider them the equivalent of a Certified Financial Planner. However, some accounting practices earn commissions from products such as insurance, mutual funds, and even stocks and bonds. Many feel that this is a conflict of interest and interferes with the accountants' presumed impartiality. This is your decision, but walk in with your eyes open.

ATTORNEYS

You may need more than one attorney. A good general attorney (here, word of mouth is also helpful) should suffice for contract reviews and most real estate transactions.

For the very important matters of estate and tax planning (wills, trusts, and so on), you should look for a specialist (in training or experience). Your trust attorney should not be handling a divorce one day and your complex wills the next. The same truth holds for asset protection issues. Look for an attorney who 1) does little else, and 2) is recommended by someone who has used his or her services.

INSURANCE AGENTS

You will most likely end up using several different insurance agents. A property and casualty agent can provide homeowners and automobile (plane, boat) coverage. A different agent usually sells health coverage. Yet another type of agent sells life insurance. In each area, a good agent is invaluable. You might choose an agent bound to a specific company (a State Farm or Allstate agent), or use an independent broker/agent who can choose from a number of companies. If your health situation is complex, a good agent can help you apply to companies that "favor" your particular condition, and help you obtain coverage that would otherwise be unavailable or more expensive. The same is true with disability insurance, especially when choosing an individually owned policy.

Dealing with a life insurance salesperson is a loaded topic. Many advisors suggest buying term life insurance and investing the difference you've saved by not buying cash-value life insurance. This pertains to the difference between cash value (whole life, variable life, universal life) and term insurance. Please see the chapter on life insurance for more detail.

ADVISOR COMMUNICATIONS

One of the frustrating aspects of dealing with your advisors is the fragments of knowledge you gain from each of them. They may give you different opinions on a topic and ultimately leave you confused. Your planner should be the one to reconcile these opinions. He or she is a translator for you, similar in behavior to a primary care physician in this regard. Your financial advisor knows your general condition and should help you understand all the input and issues you face in dealing with these other specialists. Look for a comprehensive fee-only planner. He or she is trained to tie together all aspects of your financial concerns, whereas a broker or investment manager is only interested in your investments.

REFERENCES ON WORKING WITH ADVISORS

www.CFP.net. Official site of the Certified Financial Planners Board.

www.FPANET.org. Financial planning association. Links to search engine for finding a CFP.

www.Napfa.org. The national organization for fee-only financial advisors. There are strict ethical and educational requirements to join.

12

Loose Ends

Jim Fountain turned and spoke to his friend over their dinner, "to make things worse since my divorce started, I received a notice of a potential lawsuit this week. Much of my asset protection planning was based on my being married and owning everything with Joan. Now, I'm not sure how well protected I really am anymore!"

ASSET PROTECTION FOR THE SINGLE INDIVIDUAL

*T*he ownership of assets "as tenants by the entirety" by husband and wife is especially powerful asset protection in some states (such as Florida). It is obviously not an option for the single professional, whether unmarried, divorced, or widowed. However, some other choices are available for protection from lawsuits.

For single as well as for married individuals, your qualified retirement plan is safe from creditors (federal law). In Florida and many other states, IRAs are also generally protected from business creditors. Therefore, maximizing contributions to both your qualified plan and even nondeductible contributions to an IRA make good sense for asset protection, in addition to their possible benefits for your retirement and tax planning issues. Life insurance and annuities have been a safe asset protection category in most states. Remember, however, that money put into insurance or annuities (as in qualified plans and IRAs) usually removes the ability to access the funds until later in time. This fact illustrates the basic principle that asset protection usually involves some separation between you and the assets you are seeking to protect. The more immediate control you have over the assets, the closer a creditor can get (except for ATBE ownership by husband and wife). In many states, one's homestead is very safe from attack by creditors. Therefore, consider buying a home as a method of asset protection. Other states are not nearly as generous with homestead allowances, and you need to investigate the law as it exists where you reside. It may be possible to pay off a mortgage on your home with otherwise unprotected assets when faced with a potential lawsuit. Check this with your attorney in the state where you live.

Family limited partnerships (FLP), limited liability companies (LLC), and offshore asset trusts are all available asset protection devices for single individuals. They are discussed in more detail in the chapter on asset protection. Do not rely on this book for legal advice, but be aware that some judges are beginning to pierce the protective structures of the FLPs and LLCs, especially when they are made up by a single member or when they appear to have no other legitimate purpose than as an asset protection device. There has been the suggestion that such structures with some other additional purpose involving other members of the family (FLP) or additional members (LLC) might continue to be a good asset protection tool. Offshore asset protection trusts are a highly complex and expensive device that may be useful in areas of high risk, but they must be designed and monitored by experts.

As a final comment, the reader is urged to seek competent legal counsel from an attorney on issues of asset protection. State laws differ, and the field is rapidly evolving and changing as creditors and creditor-friendly judges continue to attack protection structures.

BUYING A SECOND HOME

A second or vacation home is a common purchase by my clientele. However, it represents a large commitment of funds, and it is worth taking the time to examine a variety of aspects before making a final decision. Consider whether you and your spouse really want to go back to the same place several times a year, and then for many years. If so, the additional consideration of the cost and time involved in returning to the new dream house is next on the agenda. Although a new home in rural South Dakota may be beautiful, relaxing, and appealing, the cold reality of the climate and difficulty in reaching your retreat may temper one's enthusiasm. After passing these hurdles, you can then examine the financial issues of the second home.

The high cost of desirable and easily rentable second homes (think ski areas) almost always reflects the potential rental income. Not renting out the property is very expensive, and the income from such rentals is not a windfall, but appropriately compensatory for the inflated purchase cost. Rental income is not certain, and the cost of having the property managed from far away can easily chew up half or more of any received income. Additional financial analysis should include:

- Comparative costs of similar properties in the area.

- A careful inspection of the property, and analysis of the cost of maintenance and management of the property, regardless of potential income.

- Consideration of financing issues—how much money are you prepared to put down, and what would be the cost of the mortgage? How would this affect cash flow and ability to invest for retirement?

- A rethinking of the issues of the cost in time and travel back to the same location repeatedly over the years.

- A realistic appraisal of potential capital gain by selling the home in future years.

Next, consider the tax treatment of a rental property. If you were to rent the home out fewer than fifteen days per year, you could keep the income without reporting it to the IRS. You could deduct only mortgage interest and property taxes, but not repairs or any costs associated with the rental process. Mortgage interest deductions are limited for more expensive properties as well.

If you want to rent out the property for more than fourteen days a year, but also use it more than the same amount of time, then you would have to split the maintenance and depreciation expenses proportionally between the times allotted to personal use and to business. This is the most likely scenario for most purchasers of second homes.

If the house is used personally fewer than fifteen days a year or less than 10 percent of the days rented, then you may treat the house as a business. You could deduct all repairs, maintenance, depreciation, interest, and property taxes against the rental income—but you wouldn't be able to deduct a net loss unless your adjusted gross income was less than $150,000 a year. IRS publication 527 *(www.irs.gov/pub/irs-pdf/ p527.pdf)* has much pertinent information on the tax treatment of second homes.

Other ways to have a second home include buying into an equity-sharing or more traditional time-sharing arrangement at a resort. Owning properties with friends is also a viable choice, but fraught with personality issues.

13

Summing It All Up

"I've been reading extensively over the last few months, and I think I finally have a handle on this investing stuff," related Maria to her friend over their cocktails. "I've made a list of the ten best mutual funds from last year and I also found another article telling me the ten best stocks for 2005!" Her friend replied, "my advisor tells me not to read and believe those predictions, and I'm thrilled to leave those decisions to her."

e've covered a lot of ground in this book, and you should now have a firm start on the knowledge you need to secure your financial life. Work with some good advisors, watch your costs, and the rest should fall into place. Here are some (repeated) important truths about investing:

- You cannot beat the market. It is not clear that anyone really can, but even if you could, how would you know in advance?

- Market timing has not been proven to beat the market. Ultimately the "market" is hard to define, but what we really mean is that it is nearly impossible for an active manager to beat a passive index of stocks of the size and type that he or she invests in.

- All investors and advisors must make the active choice of asset allocation. How much should be in fixed income versus stocks? How much should be in overseas versus domestic markets? How much importance do you place on value versus growth characteristics?

- Risk is proportional to return over significant periods of time. For this reason, stocks seem risky in the short term (they are volatile), but provide the best long-term return of any asset class. Today's risk-free Treasury bill return of 1 percent actually steadily loses you money after inflation and taxes.

- Other than the last two decades in which long-term interest rates had an extraordinary fall from 15 percent to less than 5 percent, bonds are not likely to return anywhere near the rate of return of stocks. Why, then, have bonds and other fixed income in your portfolio? The current rationale for bonds is to be diversified in the event of a catastrophic market fall. When interest rates move up, bonds will become more attractive on an income basis.

- Your portfolio should contain a diverse group of investments that do not all move the same way in response to market and economic forces (that is, they are poorly correlated with each other). This diversity implies that you always have some parts of your portfolio going up and some going down, smoothing out your total return. Diversification actually allows you to choose some particularly risky investments (think emerging markets) with an overall more stable and perhaps increased return than just staying with safe assets. Remember this when some parts of your portfolio are not doing well. Also, don't be upset that your portfolio didn't do as well as its strongest parts in any particular time period. That is the idea and result of having a well-balanced investment portfolio.

- It is harder to make up a loss than to lose a gain. For example, a 50 percent loss requires a 100 percent gain just to return to your original investment. Add in inflation, loss of income, and investment costs, and a 50 percent decline may take significantly more than a 100 percent return the next year just to break even.

- Most actively managed mutual funds are not cost effective. You are paying anywhere from 1 percent to 5 percent more in yearly costs for an active management style, and are statistically unlikely to beat the index the manager invests in. Instead, buy an index fund or exchange-traded fund in the same proportional amount as the mutual fund you are considering. However, recognize that some asset classes do not have an index fund equivalent readily available.

- Real estate should be in your portfolio, but probably already is present with home and/or office ownership.

- Commodities make a good noncorrelated asset, but are generally hard to invest in. You will probably lose money investing in commodity futures. Some mutual funds are beginning to invest in natural resources, and this asset class should be on your list of considered investments.

- How long you have to invest is a crucial concept. Your time horizon for investing does not end at retirement. In fact, it ends only with the death of the last spouse or dependent who relies on you. If you are in your fifties, you have another four to five decades in which to invest. This lengthy time horizon actually is an advantage, as it allows some smoothing out of the natural volatility in riskier assets.

- You will lose money in almost any form of options trading (except for selling covered calls in some instances).

- Beware the costs of broker-sold life insurance. Make sure you are getting value for the large commission you are paying. Consider no-load products or term insurance.

- Strongly consider paying a fee-only advisor to help you.

- Watch your investing expenses. In the expected low-return environment for the next several years, expensive products can severely hurt you.

- Buy collectibles for enjoyment, not for investments.

- Network marketing schemes won't make you money.

- "Make" 10 to 18 percent a year by not carrying a balance on your credit cards.

- Always consider the taxes on any investment decision.

- Self-insure as much as possible. Use insurance for potential huge losses, not for more common small losses. Raise your deductibles until it hurts.

Index

I hope you will benefit from this book, and I would be happy to hear from you or answer questions at *Steve@WealthCareLLC.com*.

About the Author

Steven Podnos, MD, MBA, CFP®, has enjoyed diverse careers over the span of his lifetime. While working as a successful specialist in Respiratory Medicine, he also invested successfully in stock and real estate markets over two decades. From this, he realized the importance of continuing to build and preserve the wealth that he was accumulating. In a quest to do this intelligently and wisely, he began to educate himself in more aspects of investing and financial planning. Finding this process fascinating, he made the leap from helping people with their physical health to assisting them with their fiscal health.

To enhance his knowledge and expertise, Dr. Podnos proceeded to earn an MBA degree and went on to achieve Certified Financial Planner® certification. His prospering private practice in financial planning plus his own investment endeavors have created a wealth of experience in all aspects of investing for affluent individuals. He created Wealth Care LLC, to provide his clients with a method for building and preserving their own wealth. Dr. Podnos and his wife live in East Central Florida with their three teenage children.

Contact:
Steven Podnos MD, MBA, CFP®
Steven@WealthCareLLC.com
(321) 543-1099
www.WealthCareLLC.com